The Sportsman's Cookbook

FISH AND GAME

MRS E. M. WALKER

Hutchinson/Stanley Paul, London

Hutchinson/Stanley Paul & Co. Ltd
3 Fitzroy Square, London W 1 P 6 J D

An imprint of the Hutchinson Publishing Group

London Melbourne Sydney Auckland
Wellington Johannesburg and agencies
throughout the world

First published 1978
© E. M. Walker 1978

Drawings © Hutchinson/Stanley Paul & Co. Ltd
1978

All photography by Gina Harris

Set in Monotype Garamond

Printed in Great Britain by litho at
The Anchor Press Ltd and bound by
Wm Brendon & Son Ltd, both of
Tiptree, Essex

ISBN 0 09 134320 8

Contents

Foreword by Maurice Wiggin   6
Acknowledgements   6
Introduction   7

Part 1 . Fish

Introduction   13
1 Salmon and Trout   15
2 Smoked Fish   31
3 Shellfish   34
   Lobster – Crab – Crayfish –
   Oysters – Scallops – Mussels –
   Prawns – Shrimps – Scampi
4 Carp and Pike   55
5 Smaller Freshwater Fish   69
   Barbel – Bream – Char – Chub –
   Dace – Flounder – Grayling –
   Gudgeon – Mullet – Perch – Pike –
   Zander – Roach – Tench
6 Eels   91

Part 2 . Game

Introduction   101
7 Large Game Birds   105
   Pheasant – Partridge – Grouse –
   Capercailzie – Blackcock – Ptarmigan
8 Small Game Birds   117
   Woodcock – Snipe – Quail –
   Plover – Landrail
9 Wild Fowl   123
   Wild Duck – Widgeon – Teal –
   Wild goose – Cormorant – Swan

10 Pigeons and Rooks   131
11 Venison   137
12 Hare and Rabbit   145
13 Game Miscellanea   159

**Part 3 . Accompaniments to
Fish and Game**

Sauces   170
Wines   181

Appendix:
Home freezing of fish and game   185
Index   191

Foreword

6 Mrs E. M. Walker is one of the most remarkable ladies I have known, in a life devoted to the study and cultivation of remarkable ladies. She is an 'original', in the original sense of that term – a one-off, very much her own woman, highly individualistic, though not in the least eccentric (unless it be regarded as eccentric to run a sizable engineering firm very successfully while at the same time entertaining, feeding and stimulating a catholic variety of devoted friends at her beautiful ancient house). In one sense we might say that she anticipated Women's Lib; in another, she makes Women's Lib seem an anaemic and irrelevant movement.

I came to know this doyenne of the art of living through my friendship with her son, the celebrated and most inventive angler, Richard Walker, and realized in a flash where he got his originality from. To dine at her table, on beautifully cooked traditional English food, such as the traditional English sportsman brings home, was to experience a rare sense of privilege: for the conversation was as good as the food, and the music that followed, which we made ourselves, set the seal on an unforgettable evening.

Phenomenally energetic, intelligent, decisive – yet withal a reassuring and compassionate practitioner of the subtle art of friendship: this is the altogether exceptional lady whose first book I am so happy to introduce. She has lived a long life with courage and panache; she has shown us that exquisite good taste is not incompatible with resourceful practicality. 'They don't make them like that any more.'

MAURICE WIGGIN

Acknowledgements

I would like to express my grateful thanks to Fred Buller, Dr Mollie Christie, Bob Feetham, Don Griggs and Tim Daniels, Jack Hargreaves, Wilson Stephens, Fred Taylor, Jack Thorndike, Maurice Wiggin and the other kind friends who have contributed, directly or indirectly, to this book. Also to my daughter-in-law, Patricia Marston Walker, for lending me her precious first edition of *The Accomplish't Lady's Delight*.

Introduction

There is nothing so difficult as
a beginning unless perhaps, the end.

Byron

A never-ending stream of cookery books pours out from publishers, some written by Cordon Bleu experts or well-known chefs, some of absorbing interest, others rather commonplace. The majority are written by women, although Samuel Johnson pontificated: 'Women can spin very well, but they cannot write a good book of cookery.' Which perhaps is why, when I mentioned to a gathering of family and friends that I was going to write a cookery book, the news was greeted first by a stunned silence, followed by hoots of derision.

Probably because, for most of my adult life, I have been successful in the engineering industry, it is automatically assumed that I am completely ignorant of all things domestic, including cookery.

Not so, but far otherwise. My early years were spent on a farm, and few, if any, of present labour-saving devices were available. From an early age, all members of the family were expected to make themselves useful. Small girls naturally gravitated towards the household and cooking, while boys were given chores around the farm. Shopping was confined to a weekly trip to the nearest town for supplies which, in the case of meat and bread, ran out after three days, there being no refrigerators or deep-freezers. This usually meant home-made bread and emergency rations, such as bacon and onion dumpling, egg and onion pie, or dishes made from hares, rabbits, pigeons, rooks or whatever my father could 'win' with his gun. I can, in fact, claim to have given my first cookery demonstration when I was five years old. A family with a

small daughter about my own age had come to live at a cottage up the lane and our parents thought we would be nice playmates. To me, she seemed pretty dim. I was accustomed to taking part in the more robust activities of my brother (four years older) and his chums. However, one day I came across a discarded, rusty frying pan, which gave me a bright idea. I found an old bucket, filled it with paper, twigs, etc., searched the hedges till I found an egg, and having 'cleaned' the pan with a wisp of grass and water, a little of which was left in the pan, I obtained matches, lit my 'stove' and proceeded to demonstrate how to break an egg, by tapping it on the side of the pan, and then how to cook it. We had to wait till the fire died down and the pan cooled down before eating the egg. Alas! That little sneak told her mother, who told my mother and I got a sound spanking. And I never did find out whether the punishment was for fear of fire, poisoning or the waste of a good egg.

Later we moved to a farm nearer a town where my brother and I went to new schools. This opened up new interests, both my parents loved music (and both played instruments), so parties were frequent and food preparation meant a lot of cooking, in which I had to do my share.

So when I eventually married, with all the conceit of youth, I thought I could cook. But pride goes before a fall. My father brought me a hare, which he had shot, skinned and paunched for me, so I decided on jugged hare. I had no cookery book, but I knew the essentials. And I vaguely remembered that I had seen my mother add some stout (or was it port wine?) to the stock. Both were available, so I enriched the gravy with a liberal supply of each. The result was out of this world and, for a time, so were we. That was the fastest-moving hare I have ever encountered and the last I cooked for over two decades. But, *experentia docet*.

Time relentlessly marched on and once more I became involved in industry, although I spent much of my weekends making meals and baking bread.

Over the years I learned new methods, new dishes, and collected recipes from friends and relatives scattered around the world. From Aunt Lilian, married to a French hotelier at Chamonix, from Cousin May, with years of managerial experience in the restaurant of a famous store, from Adi in Austria, from Elsa who came to live with me from Germany, where she had held administrative posts in some of that country's first-class hotels, as well as from friends in Australia, New Zealand, South Africa, America, Canada and the West Indies.

I also acquired valuable knowledge from one who was a master of his craft, my friend John Fothergill, author of *An Innkeeper's Diary*. He was a dispenser of delectable dinners and luscious lunches at The Spread Eagle at Thame, which he made famous.

John, alas, no longer with us, was a great individualist who aimed for perfection in food, service and surroundings. Appreciation of his efforts meant more to him than money. But woe betide any who fell short of his high standard of morals and manners. He would show his displeasure in no uncertain terms.

He insisted on Scotch (Aberdeen Angus) beef and Welsh mutton and obviously agreed with George Borrow, who wrote: 'The leg of mutton of Wales beats the leg of mutton of any other country.' John aimed to cook the mutton he had had sent from Lake Vyrnwy (now a reservoir), in Montgomeryshire, as Borrow described it – 'rich, but delicate, replete with juices derived from aromatic herbs and cooked to a turn'.

He had many original ideas; his cooking was superb and attracted epicures and gourmets, not only from around the district but from far afield. Pages of his book listing his clients might be extracts from Debrett.

Nevertheless, during a period when circumstances took me often his way, he always gave me a warm welcome and would even ask for my opinion or suggestions regarding some new concoction.

But what prompted me to write this book was the shocking discovery that my son, Dick Walker, who is quite famous as an angler and angling author, was taking home to his first wife beautiful rainbow trout which were cooked for the cats, the family being under the impression that freshwater fish tasted muddy and were unfit for human consumption. It was only after he had lunched at my home one day and enjoyed the 'salmon' so much, and, like Oliver Twist, asked for more, that I confessed that I had, literally, 'poached' the trout he had brought along (and left behind) the evening before. His reaction was that if fish could be cooked like that, I ought to tell people how it is done. I did write a brief article, 'Cooking the Catch', which was published in an angling magazine; but I have met and still meet many huntin', shootin' and fishin' sportsmen and it amazes me how they can spend vast sums on their gear, guns and tackle and yet not enjoy the fruits of their labours. But few sportsmen nowadays cook over a campfire or, even if they have a tent or a caravan, want to spend much time cooking. Even Fred Taylor, champion camp organizer and cook – who, with two or three gas rings and a non-stick frying pan, used to produce gourmet meals from local flora and fauna (such as freshly gathered mushrooms fried with bacon) – enjoys home cooking best. And at home, maybe due to the fact that domestic cooks have disappeared and the soaring cost of hotel meals makes it practically impossible to entertain one's friends by dining out, more and more people, of both sexes, are taking a keen and ardent interest in cooking.

There is also a great difference between the final results of dishes prepared from what the sportsman has brought home fresh from a shooting or fishing trip and those made from fish or fowl from the shops, where modern methods of preservation are apt to result in a considerable loss of flavour.

It's a topsy-turvy world where now a hotel in this country is actually running a cookery course, or you can spend a weekend in Dieppe, Le Touquet or Britanny learning French cuisine. In Glasgow, cookery classes are being held for retired men, which is a splendid idea: it gives them a new interest, new friendships, and is an inestimable boon to their wives, who are happy to have them usefully occupied away from home for a few hours, as well as occasionally sharing the preparation of meals at home.

History shows that restaurants were becoming popular in England before the first French one was opened in Paris about 1782, and gratifyingly named Le Grande Taverne de Londres.

It is amusing to read in the press that at two of the most popular cookery institutes in Paris, French cuisine is being taught by Englishwomen, whilst the Parisian Académie du Vin is run by an Englishman. A London travel agency will now arrange a package tour of a week in Paris which includes a course at a bilingual cooking school. It is also interesting to learn that, in that land of frogs'

legs and snails, one of the most popular French chefs, Paul Corcellet, who numbers among his customers the famous singer Charles Aznavour, serves up braised elephant trunk (tastes like ox-tongue), boa-constrictor cutlets (like young chicken), python stew, camel hump, bear-meat pâté, tiger (marinaded in red wine) and monkey with onions. However, I think a meal there would remind me too poignantly of the siege of Paris in December 1870, when the beleaguered and starving people were reduced to eating the pets they could no longer feed. A butcher (some say he was English) in the Boulevard Haussman bought up the animals from the Jardin d'Acclimatation, including two elephants (Castor and Pollux), buffaloes, kangaroos, wolves, bears and camels. And on the ninety-ninth day of the siege the most popular restaurant in Paris offered Elephant Consommé, Haunch of Wolf, Roast Bear and Camel à l'Anglaise. Whoever named the latter must have concluded that, in controlling the Suez Canal, we had a lien on a lean camel.

French chefs have always excelled in the art of culinary decoration, and I was not surprised when recently I overheard a friend, who is a very good cook, declaring, 'I always think the most important thing in cooking is the presentation.' To some extent this may be true, but I dislike dishes embellished out of recognition, smothered in oleaginous glutinous spicy sauces, which mask the true flavour of the dish. Nor do I have any appetite for dishes garnished with the heads and tails of birds or fish. I find it disconcerting to catch the reproachful eye of a cooked trout!

However, I am delighted to learn that wise and modern French chefs are now agreed on the need for gastronomic simplicity, although they say *nouveaux-riche* clients still lay too much store on the way a dish is presented. But the true gourmet likes his meals perfectly cooked and without a lot of foolish adornment.

Probably many changes which have taken place in our eating habits over the past century have been partly due to the rationing of food in two world wars and partly to the necessity to watch our weights. Whatever the causes, meals are now lighter, simpler, more digestible and certainly more beneficial to our health.

The idea of this book is chiefly how to cook the spoils of sport. As the daughter of a shooting man, wife and mother of anglers, hostess to numerous sportsmen, I have had to prepare meals of all sorts and sizes, some easy, some elaborate, some economical for the family, and others for special occasions. I have omitted saltwater fish, because in practically every bookshop you can find cookbooks which tell you how to cook and serve them. Also, the various methods of cooking meat are known to practically everybody and have been left out for the same reason.

When writing his *Guide to Cookery*, the famous French chef Escoffier admitted that many of his recipes were originally those of three famous French *chefs de cuisine*. 'But,' he said, 'I adopted, adapted and improved.' I hope the recipes which follow will inspire you to do the same because, as that other French gourmet, Anthelme Brillat-Savarin, proclaimed, 'The discovery of a new dish does more for the happiness of man than the discovery of a star.'

Part One

Fish

Introduction

Fish-dinners will make a man spring like
a flea.

Thomas Jordan

As an article of diet, fish is highly nutritious
and one of the most valuable of protein foods;
easily digested, it promotes energy and restores
tissues. It is highly recommended for slim-
ming diets, except that frying is discouraged,
because it is the most difficult form of cooking
to digest.

Perhaps the most popular saltwater fish is
the cod, which has very little fat and is said
to contain 91 per cent of body-building
material, but it is not as easily digested as
other species. Unfortunately, future supplies
may be limited if the prolific fishing grounds
off Iceland become out of bounds.

It is unfortunate that many edible fish
around our coasts are extremely ugly in
appearance and dreaded by fishermen. The
dog-fish, for example, is of the shark family
and feeds on smaller fish. In pursuit of them,
it can damage both nets and their contents.
When caught, they are killed and thrown
overboard, but I recently read of an enter-
prising merchant who buys them cheap and,
in collaboration with an equally go-ahead
partner, processes them into very good
imitations of prawns in batter.

In the markets of France, however, the
French housewives ignore their appearance
and eat them, both fresh and salted.

Although I know some famous sea-anglers,
I do not propose to use time and space on
giving recipes for cooking saltwater fish. If
you do not know how to cook cod, sole,
plaice, etc., the counters of fishmongers are
littered with pamphlets and booklets of
instruction. However, according to the Central Office of Information, there are thirty
kinds of freshwater fish, many of which can
be caught in our country and are edible.

It is, of course, essential that the fish you
cook be fresh. In these days of refrigeration
and deep-freeze, preservation is much easier
but, even so, some of the delicate flavour of
freshwater fish gets lost unless cooked within
hours. Therefore, the angler who can catch
and cook his prize promptly is twice rewarded.

At some of the big hotels on the Continent,
fish (mostly trout or carp) are kept alive in
ponds or tanks, ready to kill and cook as the
customer orders. A German friend maintains
that she has seen such fish jumping in the
frying pan – doubtless a question of nerves.

Angling is old-established and the largest
sport in the United Kingdom in which the
sportsman actually participates. In the past,
he has been largely dependent on streams,
rivers and lochs. But in recent years, new
reservoirs have been constructed and many
private owners of worked-out gravel pits have
turned them into lakes with attractive surroundings. When stocked with fish, mostly
trout, these can prove a rewarding investment.

In some of our larger cities progressive
public authorities are considering how to
adapt, for anglers, lakes which hitherto have
been merely ornamental.

Streams where coarse fish abound seldom
need restocking, since most of the fish are
returned to the water. In May 1976, Loch
Rannoch (on the road to the Isles) which
already contained pike, perch and char was, for
the first time in thirty years, restocked with
trout.

Every year the number of dedicated anglers
grows apace, and a good angler not only
enjoys the sport, demonstrating his knowledge
and skill, but also his arrival home with the
spoils. No trout obtained by mail-order will

ever equal, in beauty or flavour, the one that didn't get away, which is the kind we are now going to cook, although no hard and fast rules can be laid down because fish vary so much, both in size and flavour.

Salmon, trout, grayling and perch are the only freshwater fish which have delicate, distinctive flavours. Carp and pike are hefty monsters with plenty of flesh to make a variety of dishes.

Coarse fish are well named because the texture of the flesh is coarse, but they are edible and must not be wasted. The smaller species do not have a lot of flavour but carefully cooked with spices, condiments and savoury additions, including garlic, onions, shallots, tomatoes, peppers, mushrooms, anchovies and cheese they are very good. Tabasco, horseradish and Worcestershire sauces, mushroom and tomato ketchups, mustard (English, French or German), cayenne pepper and paprika, too, play their part. Stuff or season with parsley, chives, bay, fennel, dill, sage, basil, thyme, tarragon, sorrel, mace or nutmeg to give added character. Vegetables such as leeks, celery, carrots and spinach are excellent with them. And of course do not forget salt and pepper (preferably black and freshly ground), and the indispensable lemon. (See the individual chapters and also the sauce chapter for recipes.)

Wine is a luxurious addition, but cider or beer should not be despised.

With such a vast variety of appetizing relishes you can ring the changes, whenever and with whatever the successful angler arrives home.

However, I am giving the recipes which I have actually used or which friends have recommended and which you may like to start on before launching out on your own individual concoctions.

Allow 1 medium-sized fish, 6 to 8oz (175–225g), for each guest, a 6oz (175g) fillet or steak or 4oz (100g) of flaked fish if cooked with other substantial additions.

KEEPING THE CATCH

Ideally, fish should be eaten on the day it is caught, but even then, a lot depends on how it is handled.

It is possible to keep some kinds of fish alive by the use of a keepnet, or a stringer. Normally, however, fish have to be killed at once and put into a cool place as soon as possible.

The introduction of plastic bags has resulted in thousands of good fish being spoiled. They may be caught in the morning, put into a plastic bag, and left in the sun in a boat, or on the bank, until dusk. By the time the angler reaches home, these fish will be starting to decompose. If they are then left in the car until next morning, they won't even be fit to feed to the cat. You can buy ready-made plastic cool-boxes, but it is easy to make one. Simply line any wooden box of suitable size and its lid with expanded polystyrene, which can be bought from builders' merchants or DIY shops.

You also need some freeze-packs; these you can also make yourself by filling suitably shaped plastic bottles with car anti-freeze, keeping them in your deep-freeze till required. Put one or two in your cool-box when you start on a fishing trip.

See also Appendix (Home freezing of fish and game).

1

Salmon and Trout

The small eate sweete, the great more daintely.
The great will seethe or bake, the small will frye.
For rich men's table, serve the greater fish –
And the small are to the poor a daintie fish.

Thomas Bastard, 1598

Salmon

Salmon (*Salmo salar*) is the acknowledged king of freshwater fish, despite the fact that much of its life cycle is spent in the sea. British salmon is considered the best of all, whether it comes from the lochs and rivers of bonnie Scotland or the waters of England and Wales, although George Borrow wrote: 'The best salmon in the world is caught in the Suir, a river that flows past the beautiful town of Clonmel, in Ireland.'

Each year, in April, the Bristol channel is usually swarming with salmon awaiting a flood to take them surging up the Severn. Curiously, many salmon anglers are unaware that hundreds of these salmon are caught in baskets in the estuary before they can get very far. These wicker baskets are about six feet (two metres) long and tapered so that a salmon entering one becomes wedged. The baskets are fixed together to form batteries, or weirs, comprising from a few dozen to several hundred. The size of these weirs is determined by statutes of great antiquity, the legality of which was examined by the Salmon Fishery Act of 1865. The Act demanded proof of 'immemorial usage', and other qualifications, and the builders of those 'weirs' which met the specifications were issued with certificates. However, while the Act fixed the size and sites of those then existing to be used 'for all time', it did ensure that no new ones would be created.

The baskets, or putchers, are placed in the river each year on 15 April, and the salmon are retrieved after each tide has ebbed. The season lasts four months.

The toll of salmon is, however, less than might be supposed, because, under certain conditions, the fish seem to sense the obstruction in the flow of water and are fastidious about any pollution. It might seem a lazy way of fishing, but keeping the baskets in constant repair and placing them over slippery slime on the river bed is not easy.

Poaching of salmon is traditional and has gone on even longer, but the old man who lured a salmon or tickled a trout upstream has gone. Methods are now becoming more modern and predatory, aiming at catching fish by the hundred by devices which include stretching long strong nets at the mouths of rivers. A short time ago, it was reported in the press that local police along the Tweed had actually caught a well-known poacher. Summoned to appear in court, his wife arrived saying he was ill in bed but pleaded guilty and she was to pay any fine imposed. While the minions of the law were occupied on the case, he nipped smartly down to the river and caught two more large salmon, the sale of which not only paid his fine, but left him with a handsome profit.

Salmon has a wonderful and distinctive flavour of its own and, being good protein food, has a high nutritional value; 'as a worthy foe or a regal dish, we respect this gallant fighting fish'.

If you have been skilful enough to catch a salmon, you will want to cook it and, if possible, whole. First, of course, you must prepare it by removing fins, gills and its internal organs. If you wish to remove the scales, they will come off more easily if you pour boiling water over the fish. Unfortunately, the days of vast ovens and culinary utensils are no more and it will probably be necessary to divide the fish into manageable portions.

How you cook it depends, of course, on the size or amount of fish available and the kind of meal at which you are serving it, but, between them, these recipes should cover every eventuality.

Jack Thorndike's Recipe

That brilliant editor of *Trout and Salmon*, Jack Thorndike, when asked for his favourite recipe, elected for an epicure's simplicity and wrote:

My wife and I both come from Lincolnshire, where good food is never spoilt by over-elaborate cooking. After overcoming the most important part of the exercise by securing fish or game of prime quality, we believe it deserves to be carefully prepared for the oven and cooked in such a way as to ensure that none of its quality of taste and succulence is lost when it is served.

Nevertheless, a couple of salmon steaks cut from a choice fish and cooked very simply, can be that much more appetising if served with a parsley sauce.

That is all you have to do to provide a quick and delicious meal:

Place two middle-cut 6-oz salmon steaks (weight depends on appetite) into a fireproof dish. Put a squeeze of lemon juice on each steak, then spread an ounce of butter over them. Cover dish with lid of foil. Bake for about 15 minutes (gas mark 5), but this time will vary according to size of steaks. Garnish with lemon and cucumber slices and serve with a choice of two sauces.

My preference is for a parsley sauce, made by melting 1oz (25g) of butter in a saucepan. Then remove from heat and stir in 1oz (25g) of flour. After this, gradually add ½ pint (300ml) milk, making a smooth cream. Stir continuously over a medium heat until sauce comes to the boil. Finally add one dessertspoon of finely chopped fresh parsley (not the packet variety), a sprinkling of salt and pepper and any liquor from cooking of the fish.

An alternative sauce, and one which some people prefer to the parsley variety, is made up as follows:

After making the basic white sauce, let it cool slightly and then add the well-beaten yolk of one egg. Stir over gentle heat for three or four minutes, but do not let it boil. As before, stir in liquor from fish and finally add a dessertspoon of lemon juice, drop by drop. Make very hot without boiling and serve.

We also enjoy salmon cooked this way without a sauce, served cold with a nice salad.

You will notice that Jack and his wife come from Lincolnshire, which explains why I once heard him, in a beautiful bass voice, singing 'The Lincolnshire Poacher' with great gusto.

Overleaf are two recipes from that cherished book *The Accomplish't Lady's Delight*, written by Hannah Wolley three hundred years ago:

To Boyl a Salmon

Boiled Salmon

18 Take as much Water as will cover it, then take Rosemary, Thyme and Winter Savory, and Salt, boyl all these very well, and then put in some Wine-Vinegar, and when your Salmon is boyled, let him remain in the same Water always, until you have occasion to eat of it.

To Roast a Salmon Whole

Draw your salmon at the gills, and after it is scalded, and wash't and dry'd, lard it with a pickled Herring, or a fat Eel salted, then take about a pint of Oysters parboyled, put to these a few sweet Herbs, some grated bread, about half a dozen hard Eggs, with 2 Onions, shred all these very small, and put to it Ginger, Nutmeg, Salt, Pepper, Cloves and Mace; Mix these together and put 'em all within the Salmon at the Gills; put them into an Oven in an Earthen-pan, born up with pieces of wood in the bottom on the dish, put Claret-wine, and baste your Salmon very well over with Butter. Before you put it into an Oven, when it is drawn, make your sauce of the Liquor that is in the Pan, and some of the Spawn of the Salmon boyled, with some melted butter on the top. Stick him about with Toasts and Bayleaves fryed, take out the Oysters from within, and Garnish the dish therewith.

Here is my twentieth-century adaptation of the cooking method favoured in *The Accomplish't Lady's Delight*:

Assuming you want to serve your big fish whole, you will need a suitable fish kettle or pan (if the latter, put a plate in the bottom). Cover with water, slightly salted, and simmer very gently, allowing 10 minutes for each pound ($\frac{1}{2}$kg) and 10 minutes extra. If, however, the size of your prize prevents it being accommodated in a pan, divide it into manageable sections and allot to each, including head and tail, a large sheet of foil. Brush each sheet over with plenty of corn or vegetable oil and wrap the salmon sections securely. Drop the 'parcels' into boiling water and simmer gently as for a whole fish, but calculating the cooking time according to the individual weight of each parcel. Unwrap each piece, peel off the skin, carefully remove the backbone, then reunite the pieces, including head and tail, on a large dish. Paint over the joins with some of the sauce you have chosen as an accompaniment (see Chapter 14 for suggestions), reheat for a minute in the oven or under the grill, then camouflage and garnish with slices of cucumber, lemon or hard-boiled egg. If it is intended to be served cold, you can put the fish (wrapped) in cold water, bring to the boil and, after 10 minutes fast cooking, turn off the heat and let the water get quite cold before removing the fish. You will find it perfectly cooked and ready for skinning and boning.

Baked Salmon

If your salmon is not more than about 5lb (2¼kg), and you are cooking for a party, take off the head and tail, fins, etc., and after scaling and cleaning thoroughly, wrap it in oiled foil and bake in a moderate oven (350°F, 180°C, gas mark 4) for an hour. Unwrap and serve hot with *maître d'hôtel* butter, or cold with mayonnaise (see sauces section for both these recipes).

Steamed Salmon

We all know that steamed fish is the most easily digested and it is therefore usually cooked this way for invalids. However, salmon cutlets, buttered, laid on a plate over a pan of simmering water, covered with the saucepan lid and steamed for about 25 minutes, a squeeze of lemon added and then served with new potatoes and green peas is a simple method, simply delectable.

Grilled Salmon

A quick method is to put the steaks in a grill pan, dotting each with butter. Pour over ¼ pint (150ml) white wine (or cider), cook under a hot grill for 5 minutes, turn, baste with the liquid and grill for another 5 minutes.

This can be served with *maître d'hôtel*, butter (page 177) or a piquant sauce (page 172), and a good gardener friend advocates sorrel or green peas and new potatoes as the perfect vegetable accompaniment.
See photograph facing page 49

Coquille of Salmon

This is another very good way of using up the remains of a cooked salmon.

about 8oz (225g) cooked salmon
2oz (50g) butter
1 cup peeled shrimps
about 6 mushrooms, sliced
¼pt (150ml) consommé
salt and pepper
2oz (50g) breadcrumbs
2 tablespoons chopped parsley

Remove the bones and flake the flesh. Into a saucepan put the butter, peeled shrimps, mushrooms, consommé, salt and pepper. Simmer gently for 10 minutes, add the fish, and cook a few more minutes. Turn onto a warmed serving dish and cover with the breadcrumbs, crisply fried then drained, and garnish with the parsley. *Serves 2 as a main course, 4 as a first course.*

Coulibiac

This is one of the great Russian dishes, as deliciously unlike British institutional 'fish pie' as it is possible to be.

1½lb (600g) salmon, off the bone
6oz (175g) unsalted butter
2 onions, finely chopped
6oz (175g) long grain rice, cooked in the usual way
2 tablespoons chopped parsley
2 tablespoons chopped dill leaves
the juice of 1 lemon
nutmeg
salt and freshly ground pepper
8oz (225g) mushrooms, roughly chopped
1lb (450g) puff pastry
3 hard boiled eggs, sliced
1 egg, beaten
½pt (300ml) soured cream

First, cut the salmon into thin slices and cook it for 3 minutes or so in 2oz (50g) of the butter – just enough to firm the flesh but not to cook it through. Sauté the onions gently until soft (but not brown) in another 2oz (50g) butter, and when they are ready add to them the cooked rice, parsley, dill, lemon juice and seasonings, stirring all together to blend well.

In a separate pan, cook the mushrooms for about 5 minutes in the last 2oz (50g) butter.

Roll out half the pastry to a rectangle about 16″ × 10″ (40 × 25cm) and place it on a dampened baking sheet. Spread half the rice and onion mixture on it, leaving a good margin free around the edges. Place on top the pieces of sliced salmon, hard-boiled eggs and the mushrooms. Finally cover this with the rest of the rice.

Roll out the other half of the pastry to a rectangle of the same size. Brush the edges of the pastry round the filling with a little of the beaten egg and press the lid over the filling sealing the edges carefully by pressing down on them. Brush the pie with the remaining beaten egg and decorate it if wished with any pastry trimmings. Make a central hole for the steam to escape and insert a chimney of rolled foil or greaseproof paper to keep it open.

Bake the Coulibiac in a fairly hot oven (400°F, 200°C, gas mark 6) for ¾–1 hour. If the top browns too quickly, cover it with a sheet of dampened greaseproof paper.

Serve the coulibiac straight from the oven, with a jug of soured cream. *Serves 6.*

Salmon Ragout

For this the fish must be fresh from the water and without any scaling.

Cut the salmon into slices an inch (2½cm) thick, put into a stewpan and pour over boiling vinegar (from ¼ to ½ pint/150–300ml, according to the size of the fish). After it is well marinaded, add a shallot, a carrot and an onion, all finely chopped; a bay leaf; a sprig of parsley and dill; ½ pint (300ml) red wine; 2oz (50g) butter; salt and pepper. If more liquor is necessary to cover, add water or clear consommé. Bring to the boil, then simmer gently for about 30 minutes. Leave till cold, strain and serve with white wine sauce (page 180).

Salmon Kedgeree

In the nineteenth century, kedgeree – which is of Indian origin – was among the dishes regularly served for breakfast in country mansions. Practically any fish can be used to make it (it has been said that the tenth Duke of Marlborough at Blenheim Palace liked his made with smoked haddock and white sauce). When a friend of mine was staying with me and I happened to have salmon leftovers available to make the kedgeree, it was voted the best ever.

about 8oz (225g) cooked salmon
6oz (175g) long grain rice
salt and black pepper
cayenne pepper
2 eggs
1 medium onion, chopped
1oz (25g) butter

Boil the rice in about ½ pint (300ml) water seasoned with salt, pepper and cayenne for 20 minutes or so. Meanwhile, hard-boil the eggs, and cook the onion in a little of the butter. Next chop the whites of the eggs and sieve the yolks. Add the rest of the butter to the rice, which will have absorbed the water and become fluffy, then the onion and the chopped egg white, and finally the flaked salmon. Turn the whole out on to a hot dish and garnish with the egg yolks.

For a richer version you can make ½ pint (300ml) of *béchamel* sauce (see page 172). Allow it to cool, then add 2 beaten eggs and 2 tablespoons of thick cream. Stir this into the rice instead of the butter, heat up and serve right away. *Serves 4.*

Sweet-Sour Salmon

4 salmon cutlets
salt and pepper
2 large onions, peeled and sliced

For the sauce

½pt (300ml) cooking liquid from the salmon
the juice of 2 lemons
¼pt (150ml) white wine
3 tablespoons brown sugar
2 egg yolks

Arrange the salmon cutlets in a baking dish and season with salt and pepper. Cover with the sliced onions and just enough hot water to cover. Cover with foil or greaseproof paper and cook for 25 minutes in a preheated moderate oven (350°F, 180°C, gas mark 4). Take out the steaks, reserving the cooking liquid. Put them on a serving dish and keep warm while making the sauce.

Strain the liquid and add to it the lemon juice, white wine and brown sugar. Simmer gently for about 5 minutes.

In a bowl, beat the egg yolks, add the liquid very gradually and cook in a double boiler until thickened slightly. Do not allow to boil. Pour over the salmon and chill. *Serves 4.*

Salmon in a Blanket

about 8oz (225g) cooked salmon, flaked
¼pt (150ml) *béchamel* sauce (page 172) OR
¼pt (150ml) double cream
4oz (100g) cucumber, peeled and diced
2 teaspoons chopped parsley or dill
salt and pepper
pinch of cayenne pepper
1 tablespoon tomato ketchup
¾lb (350g) quantity puff pastry

This is another excellent way of using salmon 'remnants'. Mix together the flaked salmon with the *béchamel* sauce or thick cream, add the cucumber, chopped parsley or dill, salt, pepper, cayenne pepper and tomato ketchup.

Roll the puff pastry out to a square. Spread the mixture smoothly over it, leaving an inch (2½cm) margin all round. Brush this with water, then bring the corners to the centre, overlapping slightly, and press the edges together to seal. Bake in a hot oven (400°F, 200°C, gas mark 6) for 20–25 minutes. *Serves 6.*

If you aim to serve this at a buffet supper, you can, of course, cut out small rounds of pastry (about 3in/18cm), put a little of the mixture in the centre of each, dampen the edges, fold in half and seal to make crescent-shaped puffs. Bake in a hot oven until golden brown.

Potted Salmon

This makes an acceptable spread for sandwiches.

Flake cooked salmon (skin and bones removed). Pound in a mortar, adding gradually a good pinch each of mace, salt and cayenne pepper. Then add alternately, still beating, drops of clarified butter and anchovy essence. When you reach a nice smooth consistency, press the paste into small jars, leaving room at the top of each for a thick layer of the clarified butter.

Salmon Soufflé

This can be made with odd pieces of raw salmon, which should be minced as finely as possible.

about 12oz (350g) raw, minced salmon
salt and pepper
3 egg whites
½pt (300ml) double cream

Season the salmon with salt and pepper and fold in 1 egg white, stiffly beaten. Chill.

Beat (separately) the whites of the other 2 eggs and the double cream till thick. Fold first the cream and then the egg whites into the salmon. Turn into a soufflé dish, set in a baking tin containing hot water, and cook in a hot oven (425°F, 220°C, gas mark 7) for 20 minutes. *Serves 4 as a first course.*

Sea Trout

Sea trout is the official name for *Salmo trutta*, this most delicious of fish, but you are more likely to find it at your fishmonger's under the label 'Salmon trout'. In fact this name perfectly describes the qualities of its flesh, which combine the firmness of the salmon and the moistness of the trout with a flavour entirely its own.

Although similar in appearance and flavour to salmon, being smaller fish – weighing between $1\frac{1}{2}$ and 4lb ($\frac{3}{4}$–2kg) – sea trout can usually be cooked whole. Many salmon recipes are equally applicable to them. One large or two small sea trout make a good meal for 6 people.

Hot Baked Sea Trout

In a fireproof dish put 2 carrots, 2 onions, 2 sticks of celery, all chopped small, salt and pepper. Lay the cleaned fish, each with a bay leaf inside, side by side on the vegetables and pour over $\frac{1}{2}$ pint (300ml) red wine. Cook in a moderate oven (350°F, 180°C, gas mark 4) for 30–40 minutes.

Strain the cooking liquor into a pan and cook till reduced by about half. Mix a tablespoon of flour to a paste with the same amount of butter, add gradually to the liquor. Remove from the heat and just before serving whisk in $\frac{1}{4}$ pint (150ml) cream and pour over the fish.

The best accompaniment to this dish is new potatoes.

Cold Sea Trout with Avocado Sauce

Sea trout can also be baked like salmon, wrapped in oiled foil (see page 18). Prepare in the same way, leaving on the head and tail and dusting over with salt and black pepper. Splash over some white wine and bake for 40–50 minutes in a moderate oven (350°F, 180°C, gas mark 4). Remove the skin (unless, like some people, you like to eat it) and the backbone and serve hot with a piquant avocado sauce. To make this, take the flesh of a ripe avocado pear, mash up with a tablespoon of lemon juice, salt, a little cayenne pepper and 2 tablespoons of sour cream.

Salmon Trout in Rosé Wine Jelly

24 This is a dish for special occasions.

1 3lb (1½kg) salmon trout
2oz (50g) powdered gelatine
2 egg whites
cucumber or tarragon for garnish

For the court bouillon

1 bottle rosé wine
4 onions
2 carrots
bouquet garni (thyme, fennel, parsley, bay leaf)
salt
12 peppercorns

Make a *court bouillon* in advance by simmering for half an hour 2 pints (1 litre) of water with the bottle of *vin rosé*, onions, carrots, *bouquet garni* and salt. Add the peppercorns and cook a further 10 minutes. Let it get cold. Put the fish in a deep fireproof dish, pour over the liquid, which must cover the fish, and bake in a moderate oven (350°F, 180°C, gas mark 4) for 45 minutes. Allow the fish to cool in the liquid, remove it and take off the skin. Melt the gelatine in a little warm water. Then whip the egg whites. Strain the cooking liquid and stir in the egg whites, boil up twice (this helps to clarify it), and finally add the gelatine. Strain again. If you have a deep serving dish, put the fish in it and pour the liquid over. Otherwise, the setting jelly has to be spooned over at intervals or chilled and then chopped and used to surround the fish. Garnish with slices of cucumber or tarragon leaves and serve with mayonnaise (page 178) mixed with whipped cream and a little lemon juice. *Serves 6.*

Trout

Shall we walk in the clear caressing sunlight
To a pure mineral spring in which mottled
trout lie?

S. Beaver

After salmon, the trout is the most highly
esteemed freshwater fish and has an almost
equally delicate flavour. Indeed, Escoffier
claimed that salmon and trout were the only
fish from British rivers and lakes worth eating.

In the early years of this century, rivers
occasionally overflowed their banks when
water cascaded down from high hills like the
Pennines, and it was then a case of drop-
everything-and-make-for-the-'water', and the
fish.

Large trout can be prepared and cooked
much like salmon, but smaller ones are equally
delicious whether baked, boiled, fried or
grilled, with or without accompaniments.

For some reason, encouraged in the fishing
trade which imports large quantities of offal-
fed trout from the Continent, there is a fallacy
that white-fleshed rainbow trout are preferable
to those with pink flesh. Nothing could be
further from the truth. A pink-fleshed trout,
properly cooked, is superb. It can be – and
indeed at my own table often has been –
mistaken for salmon.

The editor of *Angling Times*, Bob Feetham,
has decided views on how he likes trout
cooked and served, and on the right accompaniments. He writes:

My favourite fish and the way I like it cooked?
This must be a trout, preferably of about 1½lb
in size, fresh from the water.

First of all, you gut it. They always seem better
cooked that way. The flavour is much more
appealing. Then sink three cuts into each side of
the body and fill these with seasoned butter. Then

wrap securely in tinfoil (not *The Times*, as this
seems to catch fire) and bake in a moderately hot
oven (about 375°F, 190°C, gas mark 5). Leave it for
half an hour and then take it out. Remove the tinfoil (the trout tastes better without it) and eat with
salad, white wine and in the company of some
splendid young bird for whom trout and wine does
something special.

'He hath indeed, a pretty wit!' One can see
why he prefers angling to shooting. And he
would appear to have the culinary 'know-how'
which enables chefs to choose the most
succulent birds.

Bob's use of tinfoil (now marketed as
aluminium foil) reminds me of the Yorkshire
mother who intended cooking her son's catch
somewhat in the same way. But she was foiled
as her foil had completely disappeared. However, the mystery was solved when her son
arrived home from a fishing foray and took
off his boots, disclosing foil-festooned feet.
'Keeps out the cold,' he said.

My good friends Drs Mollie and Kenrick
Christie, who live at Wanganui (New Zealand),
usually fish for trout at Lake Taupo, that
great and beautiful lake in the North Island,
with a Maori background, which has been
called 'Fisherman's Paradise'. There is, in fact,
a wonderful book with that title by O. S.
Hintz, who has been called the Izaak Walton
of New Zealand. There, the catch is eaten
fresh, roasted on a grill on hot stones on the
beach, but many people have smoke-houses
on their nearby property, where the fish can
be treated with smoke made from manuka
leaves.

The fish which are taken home are often
preserved, but this is a rather long process
and, in these days of the deep-freeze, hardly
worth while.

However, Dr Mollie tells me she cooks her trout (after cleaning) by cutting it into serving pieces, laying it in a baking dish, adding a couple of finely chopped onions, a few herbs, pepper and salt, equal amounts of vinegar and water to cover and cooking in a moderate oven (350°F, 180°C, gas mark 4) with the lid on till tender.

At home, I have been told of one camping angler who cleans his fish, stuffs the cavity with freshly gathered herbs, such as sorrel or water mint, and fries the fish in oil on a bed of these herbs.

Finally, he pours over a tot of brandy and sets it alight. He calls his dish Poisson Flambeau

Truite au Bleu

This recipe is only for those who can take the trout alive and, as one chef advises, 'bang their heads smartly against the table and clean them quickly, leaving the natural slime on the skin'. The slime turns to a slaty blue when the fish is cooked in this way. Use 1 small trout per person. Slip the trout into a pan containing 4 pints (2 litres) boiling water, plus 6 tablespoons of wine vinegar. Simmer about 15 minutes and serve with a Hollandaise (page 177) or similar sauce.

Truite Guichen

1 small trout per person
seasoned flour
butter for frying
lemon juice
chopped parsley
capers

Clean and scale the trout, dry and roll in seasoned flour. Fry in butter for 5 minutes, turning over at half time. Put in a hot serving dish and sprinkle with lemon juice. Stir chopped parsley and a few capers into the cooking butter and pour over the trout.

In the journal of the Fly-fishers Club, the above recipe is given, except that instead of capers, the author, who called himself Ticklebellie, recommends sprinkling the fish with dried sage. He also says, 'It is a good plan to use half butter and half olive oil, as this does not allow the fish to stick to the pan.'

I might mention here that the French Truite Père Louis is the same fried trout, but served with a sauce made of $\frac{1}{2}$ pint (300ml) cream warmed up with $\frac{1}{4}$ pint (150ml) brandy.

Trout Poretta

1 large or 4 small trout
1 small green pepper
1 small red pepper
1 medium onion
pinch of cayenne pepper
pinch of mixed herbs
4oz (100g) breadcrumbs
8 crushed black peppercorns
salt and pepper
a little olive oil
cress
slices of lemon } for garnish

Deseed the red and green peppers and chop them, together with the onion. Add a pinch of cayenne pepper and of mixed herbs, the breadcrumbs, peppercorns, salt and pepper. Mix well, cook for a few minutes in a little olive oil, then stuff the prepared trout. Put in a fireproof dish, cover and bake in a moderate oven (350°F, 180°C, gas mark 4) for 30 minutes. Garnish with cress and lemon slices and serve, if wished, with Hollandaise sauce (page 177). *Serves 4.*

I have been told by an American friend that their trout, 'taken from the icy mountain streams, deep in the heart of Texas', are cooked in this way except that they fillet the fish and then spread it with a layer of skinned and cooked tomatoes, finishing with the pepper stuffing mixture over the top.

Truites Jurassiennes

This dish comes from the French/Swiss border and is used mostly for cooking several small trout, which are carefully cleaned, leaving on the heads and tails.

4 small trout
2 shallots, finely chopped
½pt (300ml) red wine
croûtons

For the sauce

½pt (300ml) Hollandaise sauce (page 177)
salt and pepper
2 tablespoons thick cream

Lay the fish side by side in a buttered fireproof dish. Scatter the chopped shallots over them and pour over the red wine. Cover the dish and cook in a moderate oven (350°F, 180°C, gas mark 4) for 25 minutes.

Prepare ½ pint (300ml) of Hollandaise sauce. When the trout are cooked, lift them out and remove the skins. Strain the liquid, boil rapidly for about 10 minutes then add to the sauce with salt, pepper and the 2 tablespoons of thick cream. Pour this sauce over the fish and garnish with fried bread croûtons. *Serves 4.*

Mrs Beeton's Baked Trout

Mrs Beeton was very partial to forcemeat and baked her trout stuffed with a mixture of oysters, breadcrumbs, egg yolks, suet, ground mace, savoury herbs, milk, salt and pepper.

That was before the days of inflation – oysters and eggs alone would be very costly – but a simple thyme and parsley stuffing would be equally palatable.

Mursley Trout

I am indebted for this recipe to Don Griggs, who with his partner Tim Daniels runs the superb trout fishery at Church Hill Farm, Mursley, Bucks.

1 large (2–3lb/1–1½kg) or 4 small (approx.
  8oz/225g) trout, cleaned and prepared

white wine

butter

salt and pepper

To garnish: shaped lemon halves

For the stuffing

2 dessertspoons crushed green peppercorns
2oz (50g) butter
4in (8cm) piece of cucumber, peeled and
  diced
4oz (100g) white breadcrumbs
1 tablespoon chopped parsley
1 tablespoon chopped chives
juice and grated rind of 1 small lemon
salt to taste
1 egg yolk

First make the stuffing: Melt the butter in a small pan over a low heat and stir the crushed green peppercorns into the warmed butter.

Add the rest of the ingredients, bind with the egg yolk, then stuff the fish with the mixture.

Cut a piece (or pieces) of foil large enough to enclose the fish completely. Brush it with melted butter. Place the fish on this, pour over white wine and season with salt and freshly ground black pepper. Fold the foil over twice at the top and at each end to seal the juices. Cook in a moderate oven (350°F, 180°C, gas mark 4) for 20–25 minutes for the small fish, about 45 minutes for a large one, depending on the size. Serve each person with his own foil wrapped parcel. (If you are making this recipe with a large trout, take the fish out of its wrapping and bring it to the table on a warmed serving dish. Hand the juices separately in a sauceboat.) *Serves 4–6.*

A good accompaniment to this dish would be cucumber tartlets. These are simply made as follows: Peel a large cucumber and cut it into oval shaped pieces. Blanch these for 2–3 minutes in boiling water and drain them. Turn them for a few minutes in a heavy bottomed pan over a low heat with 4 tablespoons cream and a teaspoon of fresh chopped tarragon. Serve in small, 3 inch (8cm) tartlet shells, of which this quantity should fill about 4.

See photograph facing page 64.

Truite Genevoise

4 small trout
1 large onion, minced
1 carrot, minced
4 tomatoes, chopped
olive oil
bouquet garni (thyme, parsley, bay leaf)
½pt (300ml) stock
a few capers
salt and pepper
a few green olives, sliced

Cook the onion, carrot and tomatoes in olive oil in a small saucepan for a few minutes, then put into a shallow baking dish with the stock and a few capers, salt and pepper. Finally put in the well-cleaned trout, simmer for half an hour, then add several finely sliced green olives. Cook a few minutes longer, then lift the fish out on to a hot dish, remove the *bouquet garni* and pour the liquor round the fish. *Serves 4.*

For special occasions you could add fronds of fennel to the *bouquet garni* and 2 tablespoons of dry sherry (or cider) to the stock. The liquid should just cover the trout. Cook as described above. Remove the fish, strain the liquid and use some of it, thickened, as a separate sauce.

(Dispose of the *bouquet garni*, but put the vegetables back into the rest of the stock as the base for a stew made with any leftover trout.)

Thomas Barker, a well-known angler and author of the book on angling, *Barker's Delight*, in 1657 claimed 'tho I have been no traveller, I have been admitted into the most Ambassadors Kitchens that have come into England this forty years'. As regards trout he wrote, 'Make the liquor boyle with a fierce fire. First put in one trout; blow up the fire until the liquor boyle, then put in another; so do until all are in and boyled.' He became quite lyrical on the subject and brought forth the following verse:

Restorative broth of trouts learn to make;
Some fry and some stew and some also bake.
First broyl and then bake is a rule of good skill.
And when thou dost fortune a great trout to kill,
Then rost him and baste first with good claret wine;
But the calvor'd boyl'd trout will make thee to dine
With dainty contentment both the hot and the cold;
And the marrionate trout I dare to be bold.
Sauce made of anchovies is an excellent way
With oysters and lemmon, clove, nutmeg and mace
When the brave spotted trout has been boyled apace
With many sweet herbs.

He also wrote: 'Where I was born there is not a girle of ten yeares of age but can make a (trout) pie.' Here is his own recipe for it:

Barker's Trout Pie

After making a pastry of flour, eggs, butter and milk he goes on:

'The trouts shall be opened, cleaned, seasoned with pepper and salt, laid in the pie, half a pound of currants put among the fish with a pound of sweet butter cut in pieces; so close it up [cover with pastry]; when it is baked and come out of the oven pour into the pie three or four spoonsful of claret wine, so dish it and serve it to the table.'

Trout in Aspic

This Austrian dish, excellent for a cold buffet, can be prepared the day before.

1 large trout, about 3lb (1½kg)
½ teaspoon gelatine
3–4 carrots, sliced
half an onion
a few peppercorns
1 bayleaf
1 teaspoon sugar
pinch of salt
chopped parsley
handful of chopped nuts (optional)

Dissolve the gelatine in ¼ pint (150ml) of cold water. Put the sliced carrots, half onion, peppercorns, bayleaf, sugar and salt in a saucepan with 1 pint (600ml) of water. Bring to the boil and then simmer for 15 minutes. Add the fish and continue simmering for another 10–15 minutes until the fish is soft but not overcooked, adding a little water if necessary. Lift out the fish carefully so as not to break it. Place in a shallow serving dish and surround with the carrots. Strain the liquid and stir in the gelatine until it is completely absorbed. Spoon some over the fish and leave in a cool place to set. Pour the rest into a shallow dish and chill. When set, chop with a wet knife and use, with the parsley, to decorate the fish. *Serves 6.*

In Moravia, whence this dish originates, a handful of chopped nuts is added to the liquid before it is poured over the fish.

Truite Chamonix

My aunt, who lived at her husband's hotel at Chamonix, was much intrigued by the way the French chefs cooked small trout. After being cleaned, they were dipped in milk, then rolled in seasoned flour. After that they were coated with beaten egg and covered all over in ground almonds. Finally, any remaining almonds were mixed with breadcrumbs and the rest of the egg and stuffed into the trout, which were then put into a buttered heatproof dish, covered with foil and baked in a slow oven (300°F, 150°C, gas mark 2) for 30–35 minutes. Slivered almonds were fried in oil until golden brown and then scattered over the fish before serving.

Otak-Otak

Indonesians apparently achieve the impossible by removing the flesh and bones of trout while preserving the skin intact. The method was described to me by a visitor from Malaya.

Wash the trout, then beat him gently all over with the back of a wooden spoon. This will loosen his skin and then you can very carefully take out the flesh and remove the bones. Flake the flesh, or chop it, with an onion and a clove of garlic, and add some coriander seed, salt and pepper. Beat an egg and mix all together. Fry in *ghee* (clarified butter) until cooked through. Let it cool a little, then carefully insert it into the trout skin. Roll the fish in a cabbage leaf and steam over boiling water for about 20 minutes. Heat up the *ghee* again and brown the fish before serving.

2

Smoked Fish

L'appetit vient en mangeant.
Rabelais

Smoked salmon is a traditional starter to a good meal, but the price continues to leap higher than a salmon returning to the spawning redds. One can, of course, buy smoked salmon (in oil) in tins, called Lax, but this is not cheap. In fact most convenience foods are naturally more expensive than fresh or home-made, but nevertheless it is wise to keep an assortment readily available against an emergency. Such as when the secretary of an overseas golf club cabled to say he would be arriving at my home next day at 12.30 p.m. and turned up at 1.30 p.m., complete with buxom wife and two teenage daughters, and all four apparently famished.

Of course, if you are among those fortunate anglers who can often (or even occasionally) land a perfect specimen, it might be worth while smoking your own.

There are two ways of smoking salmon, trout and sea-trout: *cold smoking* and *hot smoking*. If you buy 'smoked salmon', what you get will be cold-smoked. This is done by steeping the fish, after it has been cleaned and split into two sides, in a brine bath. Some professional salmon-smoking firms use plain brine; others add sugar, or a little saltpetre and Jamaica pepper. After soaking for several hours, the sides are drained and hung in a smoke chamber, fed by the smoke from smouldering sawdust. This is usually oak, but sometimes other sawdusts are used, such as apple, cherry, ash or hickory. Evergreen and conifers must never be used, especially pine or fir, or the fish will smell and taste like turpentine.

Sea-trout and freshwater trout, both brown trout and rainbows, can also be smoked in this way, if large enough. About 4lb (2kg) is the lowest limit; anything smaller tends to become rather too dry.

Fish for smoking, as described above, can be deep-frozen while fresh, thawed, smoked and then refrozen. The smoked sides can be frozen whole, or sliced and the slices frozen in packs, each slice separated by a piece of greaseproof paper, and then the pile of slices placed in a sealed polythene bag. Packs of 4oz (100g) each are most convenient, since 2oz (50g) is a generous helping.

However, if you are having a party, it is nice to make a little ceremony of the slicing, which is easy if you know how, but impressive to those who don't. For this you need a plain clean board, a strong pair of tweezers or forceps, and a sharp knife. The best kind is what is called a ham knife, with a long, thin, narrow blade. If you do much slicing of smoked salmon or trout, it is worth buying a ham knife specially for it, and a good sharpener to go with it.

The first job is to remove the bones. Lay the fish skin-side down on the board and run the tips of your fingers over it, feeling for bone ends, each of which you then grip with the forceps. Look for the way the bone lies and pull it out endways. Keep on until you have removed all these bones. In addition to the ribs, there is another line of much smaller bones that lie straight up-and-down, as the side is lying on the board. This line of bones is between the thicker ends of the ribs and the back of the fish. Make sure you remove all these too.

Salmon and sea-trout are sometimes a little on the dry side after smoking; if so, you can rub a very little olive oil into the side, opposite the skin. Brown and rainbow trout, on the other hand, are usually very oily and you may have to mop off the surplus with paper tissues before slicing.

To slice, assuming you are right-handed,

lay the side skin-side down and tail-end (the narrow end) to your right. Hold the knife, sharp edge to the right, at right angles to the side of the fish, and take the first slice from about two inches from the thin end, slicing towards the thin end. This will produce a hard, dry slice, which we call 'the dog's bit', because the dog gets it!

Now you can remove a series of slices, working at a shallow angle, through the flesh right to the inside of the skin. Provided you don't cut directly straight down, you'll find that when the edge of your knife reaches the inside of the skin, the knife turns a little of its own accord and runs parallel to the skin, detaching the slice very neatly.

You can slice smoked salmon very thin; smoked sea-trout has to be sliced thicker, and smoked rainbow or brown trout thicker still. If you try to slice trout too thinly, the slices break up, so start them at least an eighth of an inch thick.

Hot-smoked trout is quite different. This method is used for relatively small fish, which are cleaned but not soaked in brine. Instead, they are lightly sprinkled with salt and pepper and put into a small smoking box, of which several are on sale, the famous Swedish fishing tackle firm ABU being the pioneers of *hot-smokers*. You can also obtain an aluminium smoker complete with grid, burner and oak sawdust from Habitat, Tottenham Court Road, London, or one called Optimus from the Country Gentlemen's Association Ltd, Letchworth.

These boxes come with full instructions and a bag of sawdust. A little spirit stove slides inside and provides the heat. By this method the fish is cooked and smoked at the same time; it can be eaten hot, just as it comes

from the smoker, or allowed to become cold. It needs no sauce when eaten hot; when cold, the best sauce, to most people's way of thinking, is fresh-grated horseradish and cream (see recipe, page 177).

Should you wish to know more about smoking, a book by John Seymour called *Self-Sufficiency* (Faber, 1973) – about producing and preserving your own food – gives a great deal of information and instruction about smoking both fish and meat.

It is a great mistake to think that smoking, either hot or cold, is going to make good food from poor fish. So often, when an angler catches a salmon that has been in the river for months and is marbled and reddish, you will hear someone say, 'Oh, that will do for smoking!' All it will produce is very poor quality smoked salmon. If a fish is not fit to eat when cooked fresh, it is not fit for smoking, by any method.

However, in recent years, it has been possible to have one's fish smoked by professionals for a very modest fee, which saves a lot of time and trouble. But if you are not an angler and just buy from the fishmonger, try very thin slices of raw kipper with a squeeze of lemon, in sandwiches, canapés and mousses.

Smoked salmon is usually served on a bed of lettuce with lemon slices and cayenne pepper; smoked trout with fresh horseradish and cream sauce (see recipe, page 177); and both with thinly sliced brown bread and butter. In his fascinating book about his wartime experiences in the RAF, Captain Guy Gibson vc tells how he and his wife, temporarily based in a rural public house, were sent a pack of Scotch smoked salmon. They told the landlord's wife they would have it for supper. They did – fried in batter.

Smoked Salmon Soufflé

34   6oz (175g) smoked salmon, minced
2 eggs, separated
1oz (25g) butter
1oz (25g) flour
½pt (300ml) milk
a squeeze of lemon juice
salt, pepper, paprika

Separate the eggs, beat the yolks and whisk the whites. Melt the butter over low heat, add the flour and stir till smooth; gradually add the milk, the egg yolks, lemon juice, salt and pepper. Next, mix in the salmon and, finally, fold in the egg whites. Pour into a greased soufflé dish and bake in a moderately hot oven (375°F, 190°C, gas mark 5) for 30 minutes. Sprinkle with paprika before serving. *Serves 4.*

Smoked Fish Mousse

Both smoked salmon and trout can be pounded to a paste and, with additions, made into attractive hors-d'oeuvres. A simple method is to add cream cheese (about half the quantity of fish) the juice of half a lemon, salt and pepper and just enough cream to make a stiff mousse.

An alternative, slightly more elaborate mousse, is made by pounding the yolks of 3 hard-boiled eggs with 1 tablespoon of olive oil, 1 tablespoon of tarragon vinegar, 2 tablespoons of minced beetroot, 3 tablespoons of sour cream, and a teaspoon of French or German mustard. Divide the fish into four 4oz (100g) portions, cover with the mixture and decorate with chopped egg whites and parsley.

Buttered Eggs with Smoked Salmon

This makes a fine, luxurious breakfast dish.

12 eggs
6 tablespoons cream
Salt and freshly ground black pepper
4oz (100g) butter
6oz (150g) smoked salmon, cut in strips

Lightly beat the eggs and cream together and season them with salt and pepper. Melt the butter in a heavy bottomed pan, add the eggs and cook them gently. Immediately the eggs reach setting point, fold in the smoked salmon strips, and serve immediately. *Serves 6.*

Salade Morceau

However adept you are at slicing, you will inevitably find that fragments remain. These must not be wasted. Collect them and cut any of the larger pieces into strips. To make this attractive hors d'oeuvre, mix together 4 heaped tablespoons of mayonnaise; a teaspoon each of curry powder and vinegar; 4 sticks of celery, chopped small; 4 tomatoes, skinned, seeded and diced; 2oz (50g) of boiled rice (or 2 tablespoons of white breadcrumbs), salt and pepper and finally about 4–6oz (100–175g) of smoked salmon pieces. Pile on a dish and garnish with watercress and cucumber slices. *Serves about 4.*

Egg and Salmon Patties

These are very useful for buffet parties. Mince any leftover smoked salmon. Allow 1 egg for each 1oz (25g) of fish. Scramble the eggs, and to them add salt, a little cayenne pepper and the fish. Make shortcrust pastry and roll out very thin. Cut into 4-inch (10cm) squares. Put about a tablespoonful of the mixture on each square, fold over cornerwise to make a triangle, moisten the edges and press to seal with a fork. Bake in a moderately hot oven (375°F, 190°C, gas mark 5) for about 20 minutes or till lightly browned.

Smoked Salmon Canapés

There are, of course, many other ways in which smoked salmon and trout can be eked out or leftovers used up, such as spreading pieces with crabmeat and rolling them up (securing with a cocktail stick) or adding them to tomato or cucumber slices in sandwiches. An ingenious friend makes excellent canapés this way: she soaks some slices of stale white bread in milk, drains them, sandwiches pieces of trout between each two slices, and lays them on a well-greased baking tin. She then piles grated cheese on each, dots them with butter, cooks them in a fairly hot oven (400°F, 200°C, gas mark 6) till golden brown.

Smoked Eel

In many countries, smoked eel is regarded as a special delicacy, and eels from Scotland are in great demand. I am told that the Danish Food Centre in Glasgow is regularly supplied with eels from a Monteith fishery. They can be simply served with a little horseradish sauce (see page 177) and brown bread and butter. If you catch eels and want to smoke them yourself, this is the way:

As soon as possible after being caught, the eels must be gutted, cleaned and placed in a solution of brine (5lb/2¼kg salt to 3 gallons/13½ litres of water) to which 2 tablespoons each of lemon juice and onion juice should be added, with 2 cups of demerara sugar. After the eels have been immersed for at least an hour, drain and rinse them in fresh water. Dip them into boiling water then hang them in a smoking chamber.

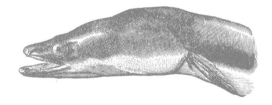

Smoked Eel Smetana

36 The composer Smetana (of *Bartered Bride* fame) is said to have preferred smoked eels to smoked salmon, and this is alleged to be his favourite recipe:

1 smoked eel
2 eggs
1 teaspoon German mustard
3 tablespoons olive oil
1 tablespoon tarragon vinegar
2 tablespoons sour cream
1 teaspoon caster sugar
salt and pepper
2 tablespoons minced beetroot

Fillet the smoked eel. Place portions on serving plates. Hard boil the eggs. Pound the yolks and mix with the German mustard, olive oil, tarragon vinegar, sour cream, caster sugar, salt and pepper. Colour with the minced beetroot. Spread the mixture over the eel fillets, garnish with the egg whites, chopped, and serve with brown bread and butter. *Serves 4.*

Earlier I mentioned salmon poachers. It would seem that even trout is now at risk, since last season three predatory characters were caught in the act at the stream which flows through the farmlands in Sussex belonging to the Rt Hon. James Callaghan. But 'all's well that ends well'; the spoils of the chase were returned to the owner 'grilled and trimmed with butter sauce, almonds and garlic on a bed of spinach'. And at a trout farm at Inverdruie, poachers are daily taking fish from right under the eye of the manager, who is helpless to prevent them. The audacious marauders are the famous Aviemore ospreys.

For the enjoyment of my angling friends, I will close this chapter with these lines from John Wolcot, written about 1788:

Enjoy thy stream, O harmless fish;
And when an angler, for his dish
Through gluttony's vile sin
Attempts, the wretch, to pull thee out,
God give thee strength, O gentle trout,
To pull the rascal in!!

3

Shellfish

Lobster demands a rare combination of
knowledge and virtue in him who sets it
forth.

Thomas Love Peacock

Lobster

It is agreed that a lobster freshly boiled is vastly superior in flavour to one purchased already cooked. Nevertheless, it is rather daunting to the tender-hearted to have to act as executioner.

For those who put flavour before fear or favour, that most famous of chefs, Escoffier, directs: 'The first essential condition is that the lobster should be alive. Select a lobster full of life and plunge it into boiling *court bouillon*.' Or, for another dish: 'Take the live lobster, sever its claws, cut the tail in sections and split the carapace in two, lengthwise.'

Some years ago, the RSPCA took up the case of cruelty to lobsters, and then came to the conclusion that if the lobster is put into *cold* water and brought to the boil slowly, it dies painlessly when the heat reaches 70°F. The matter was brought up again in 1975, but I cannot recall that any definite decision was reached.

Way back at the beginning of the century, someone considered it more humane to 'pierce the spinal cord with a sharp skewer or knife at the joint between the body and the tail shells'. And in a French book published in 1961, we are told to 'plunge the point of a knife into its head between the eyes', or 'sever the spinal cord at the juncture of the chest and tail'.

Could you gaze into his eyes and do that? If not, you must buy your lobster from the fishmonger.

If you are going to buy one ready-boiled, pinch him firmly in the tummy; if the tail springs back, you have a desirable specimen. Personally, I am at present 'off' lobster. It has been my lot in life to entertain, or be entertained, at lunches or dinners in hotels throughout Great Britain, and only twice have I had to send any food back as uneatable. In both cases, it was lobster. At a famous West End hotel, I ordered Lobster Newburg and at a hotel in the Home Counties, I chose Lobster Thermidor. In each case, the lobster meat was so tough, it was like trying to chew solid rubber. Since then I have eschewed lobster. However, next time I fancy Lobster Newburg or Lobster Thermidor I will make my own, in my own way, which will not be so elaborate as Escoffier's presentation.

Speaking generally, it is usual to allow half a lobster per person for a main dish, but lobster meat can be eked out in many ways and still retain its unique flavour.

Lobster Thermidor

2 lobsters
1 onion, quartered
2 peppercorns
1 bay leaf
sprig of thyme
pinch of salt
½pt (300ml) milk
2oz (50g) butter
1oz (25g) breadcrumbs
1oz (25g) grated Parmesan cheese

For the sauce

2 tablespoons flour
¼pt (150ml) dry white wine
1 egg yolk
1 teaspoon lemon juice
1 teaspoon French mustard

Put the onion in a saucepan with the peppercorns, bay leaf, thyme, a pinch of salt and the milk. Bring to the boil, remove from heat, cover and leave to infuse.

Chop the meat from the shells and claws of the lobsters – you should have about 1lb (450g) – and fry in half the butter for about 5 minutes. Make a thick sauce with the remaining butter, the flour, the infused milk and some white wine, then add the egg yolk, French mustard, salt, pepper, lemon juice and cream. Cook for about 5 minutes, but do not allow to come to boiling point. Stir in the fried lobster.

This is usually served in the lobster shells, with the breadcrumbs mixed with grated Parmesan cheese sprinkled over and then put under the grill or in a hot oven till the cheese browns. *Serves 4.*

Lobster Newburg

2 lobsters
4 slices white bread
2oz (50g) butter, melted
2 tablespoons dry sherry
1 tablespoon brandy
3 egg yolks
3 tablespoons double cream
paprika

Having extracted the meat from the lobsters, cut it up into fairly large pieces. Dip the slices of white bread into the melted butter, drain off surplus and put them on a baking sheet in a warm oven to crisp up. Cook the lobster in butter for a few minutes over low heat; add the sherry and brandy. Beat together the egg yolks and double cream. Pour this over the lobster, mix carefully so as to avoid breaking the lobster pieces, then spoon onto the toasted bread slices, dust with paprika and serve. *Serves 4.*

Homard à la Greque

1 lobster
2 onions, sliced
1 wineglass olive oil
½lb (225g) tomatoes, chopped
salt and pepper
1 tablespoon chopped parsley
1 glass white wine

Sauté the sliced onions in a little of the olive oil, add the chopped tomatoes and parsley and season with salt and pepper. Pour in the glass of white wine and the rest of the olive oil. Bring to the boil and add the lobster meat, cut up. Mix well, reduce heat and simmer until fairly thick. *Serves 4.*

Lobster or Crab Sauce

If you buy cooked lobsters or crabs in their shells, the latter can be used to make a good flavouring sauce. Dry the shell in the oven, then pound to a powder in a mortar. Add a half teaspoon of paprika to each medium sized shell and fry for a few minutes in hot butter. Add a little water, bring to the boil, stirring, then set aside to cool. When cold, the fat should be taken off the top, and the sauce put into a screw-top jar and kept in the refrigerator.

Lobster Ramekins

1 lobster
2oz (50g) butter
4oz (100g) white breadcrumbs
salt and freshly ground black pepper
cayenne pepper
nutmeg
lemon juice
2oz (50g) grated Swiss cheese

Melt the butter in a heavy pan over low heat, and stir in the lobster meat, chopped. Add the breadcrumbs, salt, pepper, a pinch of cayenne and nutmeg, and mix all well together. Add lemon juice to taste.

Preheat the grill and fill 6 ramekins or other small flameproof dishes with the mixture. Sprinkle over the grated cheese and brown under the grill. Serve right away. *Serves 4 as a first course.*

Lobster Mousse

1 lobster
1 leek, sliced
a few sticks of celery, sliced
2–3 carrots, sliced
salt and pepper
gelatine
½pt (300ml) cream
cucumber
tomatoes } for garnish
hard-boiled egg

Chop the lobster meat. Cook the vegetables in about ¾ pint (450ml) water till tender; add salt and pepper. Drain and set aside. Boil the cooking liquid till reduced to ½ pint (300ml). Melt sufficient gelatine to set this quantity, and add to it the whipped cream and reserved vegetables and lobster. Put in a mould and chill until set. Turn the dish out onto a serving dish on a bed of lettuce leaves, and garnish it. *Serves 6.*

Homard à l'Américaine

This method of presenting lobster is very popular for special occasions in France, although it apparently originated in America. Each of the two countries has its own version of this classic dish. Both recipes start off in the same way, by stipulating that the lobster should be alive and killed just before cooking, but whilst the French don't give instructions on this matter, my American friends just tell one laconically to sever his spinal cord, slice him in half from head to tail, remove the black line and stomach, and reserve the coral.

Put in a deep pan a tablespoon of butter and 4 tablespoons of oil, heat gently and, when melted and fused, put in the lobster and watch it gradually turn red before your very eyes. Now here is where America and France differ:

AMERICAN RECIPE

In America, at this point, the lobster is sprinkled with a chopped onion, a dash of cayenne pepper, a pinch of thyme and a small bay leaf. Cover and cook for about 5 minutes, then add 2 tablespoons tomato paste mixed with 2 tablespoons dry white wine. Cover again and cook over low heat for 15 minutes. Then take out the lobster, put in the coral and boil up till thick and serve with the lobster. If more than 2 people are dining, the meat is taken from the shells and divided. On special occasions, a wine glass of brandy is warmed, poured over the lobster and set alight.

FRENCH RECIPE

In France the herbs are omitted, but when the lobster (cooking in the butter and oil) begins to turn red, a wineglass of brandy is poured over and set alight. When the flame has died down, the pan is covered, the cooking continued for about 5 minutes, then the brandy sousing and flambé is repeated; and yet a third time! Meanwhile a sauce is made by mixing 1 tablespoon each of minced onion and chervil with the juice of a lemon, 2 tablespoons of tomato sauce and $\frac{1}{2}$ pint (300ml) good stock. This is heated up, the coral added and, when blended in, served with the lobster.

Lobster Bisque

42 8oz (225g) lobster meat *or*
    4oz (100g) lobster and 4oz (100g)
    peeled prawns
oil for sautéing
1 small tin clams (optional)

For the sauce

6 tablespoons butter
1 tablespoon curry powder
6 tablespoons flour
1½ pints (900ml) hot milk
4 tablespoons shallots or onions, chopped
salt and pepper
parsley

Melt the butter over low heat, stir in the curry powder and flour and cook to a *roux*, then add the hot milk, chopped shallots or onions, salt and pepper.

In another pan, sauté the lobster meat (or the lobster and prawns) for a few minutes in a little oil. If you have a tin of clams, drain the contents, reserving the liquid. Add the clams to the lobster, cook for a few minutes more, pour over the clam juice, mix well, then combine with the white sauce and reheat. Sprinkle with chopped parsley and serve. *Serves 6.*

Lobster au Gratin

1 lobster
a few mushrooms, sliced
1 large onion, peeled and sliced
a little oil for frying
1oz (25g) butter
1oz (25g) flour
½pt (300ml) milk
salt
pinch cayenne pepper
1 tablespoon fried breadcrumbs
1 tablespoon grated cheese

This is one of the easier methods of serving lobster. Remove the meat from the shell and claws and cut into neat pieces. Fry the mushrooms and onion in a little oil. Meanwhile, make a thick *béchamel* sauce with 1oz (25g) butter, 1oz (25g) flour and the ½ pint (300ml) milk. Season with salt and a pinch of cayenne pepper and put in the lobster and mushroom and onion mixture. This can then be piled into the lobster shells or on to a fireproof dish. In either case, sprinkle over a tablespoon of fried breadcrumbs mixed with a tablespoon of grated cheese and brown quickly under the grill. *Serves 3–4.*

In South Africa a somewhat similar dish is made by using the white sauce and lobster (kreef) baked. First the bottom of a casserole is covered with the sauce, then a layer of lobster meat, seasoned with salt and cayenne pepper, and then a sprinkling of chopped parsley and breadcrumbs is added. These layers are alternated until the dish is filled, ending with a layer of sauce. The top is then sprinkled with breadcrumbs, dotted with butter and the dish quickly browned under the grill.

Crab

Although crab is considered inferior in quality and flavour to lobster, where the latter is not available crab can be successfully substituted. Some lucky people are able to obtain their crabs straight from the sea but they are usually bought ready-cooked. Some fishmongers will, if requested, dress them, but, should you find it necessary, you can easily tackle this job yourself:

To dress a Crab

If your crab is fresh, first wash it and put it in a large pan with plenty of cold water and salt. Cover, bring to the boil and simmer for 15–20 minutes. Remove from the pan and leave to cool.

When the crab is cold place it on its back on a board and twist off the legs and two large claws. Remove the pointed flap and take out and discard the greyish-white stomach sac which lies behind the head and the grey feathered gills or 'dead men's fingers'.

Spoon out all the soft, yellowish-brown meat from the shell and put it in one bowl. Crack open the large claws, remove the pinkish-white meat and put it into another bowl. In the same way, crack open and remove the remaining meat from the legs and scrape out any residual fibres clinging to the body shell.

A 2–2½lb (1–1¼kg) crab should yield 1lb (450g) meat, enough to serve 4 people. The empty shell makes an attractive container and some people prefer to serve it this way, with a fresh green salad and mayonnaise (page 178).

So many crab recipes are similar to lobster, to give them would be vain repetition so I am giving here just a few of my favourite ones.

Crab Mousse

8oz (225g) crab meat
1 tablespoon grated Parmesan cheese
salt and pepper
squeeze of lemon juice
¼pt (150ml) aspic jelly
⅛pt (75ml) double cream
2 egg whites, beaten

Mix the crab meat with the grated Parmesan cheese, season with salt and pepper and lemon juice. Add the aspic jelly (cool, but not set) and double cream. Set aside in a cool place for an hour, then fold in the 2 whisked egg whites. Put into a soufflé dish and chill in the refrigerator. *Serves 4 as a first course.*

Devilled Crab

1lb (450g) crab meat
2 hard-boiled eggs
2 tablespoons chopped parsley
1 medium onion
1 small green pepper
1oz (25g) grated cheese
1oz (25g) breadcrumbs
1oz (25g) butter

For the sauce

1oz (25g) butter
1oz (25g) flour
½pt (300ml) hot milk
2 tablespoons Worcestershire sauce *or*
  a few drops Tabasco
1 tablespoon French or German mustard
salt and pepper
½ teaspoon cayenne pepper

Chop the hard-boiled eggs, parsley, onion and green pepper. To make the sauce, melt the butter, stir in the flour and gradually add the hot milk. Bring to the boil, stirring, and simmer for 5 minutes. Add the remaining ingredients. Stir in the crab meat, put in a fireproof dish (or, for a party, in small ramekins). Sprinkle with a mixture of the grated cheese and breadcrumbs, dot with butter and bake in a hot oven (400°F, 200°C, gas mark 6) for 20 minutes. *Serves 4 as a first course.*

Crab Soufflé

8oz (225g) crab meat
3 tablespoons minced onion
a little butter
½ cup (150ml) white sauce (made from
  1 tablespoon flour, 1 tablespoon butter,
  ½ cup milk)
½ cup cream
½ cup boiled rice
½ cup tomato purée
½ cup white breadcrumbs
1 teaspoon curry powder
salt and pepper
cayenne pepper
3 eggs, separated

Fry minced onion in butter till softened, then add the crab meat, white sauce, cream, boiled rice, tomato purée, white breadcrumbs and curry powder. Season with salt, pepper and a pinch of cayenne. Bring to the boil, add 3 well-beaten egg yolks, and cook for a few minutes, stirring rapidly, but do not allow to approach boiling point again. Remove from heat, cool, and then fold in the stiffly beaten egg whites. Put into a well-greased soufflé dish, stand in a baking dish of hot water in a moderate oven (350°F, 180°C, gas mark 4). Cook for 45 minutes and serve *instanter. Serves 4 as a first course.*

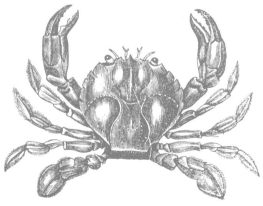

Crayfish

This small crustacean can still be found in many of our rivers, but a considerable number are needed to make a meal since only the claws and tail yield meat. About 3lb ($1\frac{1}{2}$kg) will give sufficient for 4 servings of the recipes below. (Do not confuse it with crawfish which is a species of lobster found around our south-western coasts.)

They must be plunged into boiling, very salty water to kill them, then removed immediately. At the tail-end there are seven lobes (or fins). Take the centre between thumb and forefinger, give a sharp twist (through 180 degrees) and pull hard. This will remove the intestine.

Boil the crayfish again in fish stock or lightly salted water, this time for 10–15 minutes, then take them out, drain, shell and dry. Sauté the meat in butter for a few minutes, stirring and turning. Pour over a glass of warmed brandy and set it alight. Divide into individual bowls.

Mix a little of the stock with the frying butter, pour over and sprinkle with minced fresh herbs.

Crayfish Cocktail

This makes a delightful hors d'oeuvre for 4 people.

about 24 crayfish
court bouillon (see page 48)
mayonnaise (page 178) flavoured to taste with french mustard, tomato purée, and the juice of about $\frac{1}{2}$ lemon
young lettuce leaves

Clean the crayfish, gut and wash them under running water. Boil them in the court bouillon for 5 minutes. Leave them to cool in the liquid, then shell them, but leave 4 unshelled for decoration.

Gently mix the crayfish into the mayonnaise.

Line the bottom of 4 wide, long-stemmed glasses with lettuce leaves, and divide among them the dressed crayfish.

Finish by decorating each one with an unshelled crayfish.

Bateaux D'Ecrevisses

After boiling the crayfish the second time as described above, cut them in half down the middle and take out the flesh, reserving the shells (carapaces). Mince the flesh, add an equal amount of breadcrumbs, and season with salt and cayenne pepper. Fry in 2oz (50g) of butter until the breadcrumbs are crisp and golden. Fill the shells and spoon over each a little cream dusted with paprika.

Oysters

46 Oysters have always been considered a great delicacy, but except in districts where there are oyster beds, and in London and other big towns, where there are oyster bars, one seldom sees oysters for sale. It is of course unwise – and unsafe – to eat them unless they are perfectly fresh. They are in season whenever there is an 'r' in the name of the month.

To open Oysters

First, scrub the closed shells well to remove all sand. Before picking up the oyster, wrap your left hand in a clean tea towel. Hold the oyster in the palm of the hand, flat side uppermost. Slip an oyster knife or a short, wide-bladed kitchen knife into the hinge. Twist the knife to prise open the hinge and cut the muscles which lie above and below the oyster. Finish by freeing the oyster from its base. Discard the flat shell and serve as suggested below.

The simplest methods of serving oysters are generally the best. Usually they are eaten raw, allowing 6 oysters per person. Each one is placed on the deep half of its shell and embedded in a dish of crushed ice, sometimes decorated with a little seaweed. Some people like a squeeze of lemon juice, others wine vinegar or a dash of cayenne pepper, but the connoisseur just swallows them unadulterated.

Oysters au Gratin

oysters
minced herbs (parsley, chives, thyme)
lemon juice
breadcrumbs
melted butter

Detach the oysters from their shells, leaving them in the concave half. Sprinkle over each minced herbs, lemon juice, breadcrumbs, and finally melted butter. Brown them under a hot grill for 3–4 minutes and serve straight away in the shell.

Angels on Horseback

Still others prefer oysters cooked. In this favourite method you simply wrap each oyster in a thin rasher of bacon, fix with a toothpick and grill for a few minutes.

Scallops

Although they are in season in January and February, scallops have become increasingly expensive and unobtainable, except frozen, when the flavour seems to have evaporated.

They can be cooked like lobster, but I include a few of the most successful ways I know of cooking this delicate and delicious shellfish.

To prepare fresh scallops for cooking

First, scrub the closed shells in cold water and place them, flat side down, in a pan over high heat, shaking them, for a few minutes, to open them. Discard any unopened shells. Next, slip the blade of a knife between the two half scallop shells and cut through and remove the hinge muscle. Detach the rounded shells, clean them and keep them for later use. (They make excellent containers for hors-d'œuvres and other small dishes.)

Next, scrape away the beard-like fringe from around the scallop, slide the blade of the knife under it and ease off the white flesh with the coral attached.

Cook according to the instructions given in the following recipes.

First, the acknowledged classic scallop recipe:

Coquilles Saint-Jacques à la Provençale

1 onion, chopped
2oz (50g) butter
1 clove garlic, chopped finely
12 large scallops or their equivalent
seasoned flour
olive oil
¼pt (150ml) dry white wine
small bay leaf
pinch of thyme
1oz (25g) swiss cheese, grated

Cook the onions in half the butter over low heat until soft. Add the garlic and cook another minute or so. Set aside.

Slice the prepared scallops. Roll in the seasoned flour and shake off the excess. Heat the rest of the butter and a little olive oil and sauté the scallops over a high heat until lightly browned. Pour the wine into the pan, together with the onion and herbs. Simmer for 5 minutes to reduce the sauce and thicken it slightly.

Remove the bay leaf and divide the scallop mixture into 6 small dishes or shells. Sprinkle over the grated cheese, dot with more butter and put under a hot grill until golden brown. *Serves 6 as a first course.*

Buttered Scallops

48 8oz (250g) scallops
5oz (125g) butter
a little olive oil
chives, parsley, basil (or thyme), finely
    chopped

Slice the scallops and sauté them in 1oz (25g) of the butter and a little olive oil. Remove from the pan and put in warmed shells or small dishes. Keep hot.

Melt the remainder of the butter and mix into it the finely chopped herbs. Pour this over the hot scallops and serve immediately with lemon quarters and brown bread.

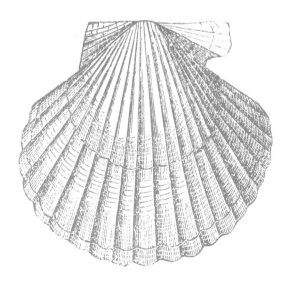

Stafford Scallops

12 large scallops
8oz (250g) button mushrooms, sliced
6oz (175g) butter
1 tablespoon flour
2 egg yolks
breadcrumbs
For the court bouillon
½pt (300ml) dry white wine
⅛pt (75ml) water
sprig of thyme
½ bay leaf
1 onion, finely chopped
pinch of salt and pepper

Prepare the scallops as described on page 47, reserving the concave lower shells.

Poach the scallops in the *court bouillon* for 5 minutes. Drain, reserving the liquid, and cut into thin slices.

Sauté the sliced mushrooms in 2oz (50g) of the butter for a few minutes, add the cooked scallops, cover and set aside.

In a saucepan melt another 3oz (75g) butter, add the tablespoon of flour and cook for a minute or two to make a *roux*. Add gradually to this the strained *court bouillon*. Bring to the boil and simmer for a few minutes, stirring, to make a smooth sauce.

Mix the 2 egg yolks with a little of the sauce, then add this to the remainder, off the heat. Return to the heat and cook, stirring, till thickened, but do not allow to come to boiling point. Finish with the final 1oz (25g) butter and check the seasoning.

Place a spoonful of the sauce in each of the 6 scrubbed scallop shells, then divide among them the cooked scallops and mushrooms, together with the coral. Cover with the remaining sauce, sprinkle with breadcrumbs and put under a hot grill for a few minutes till golden brown. *Serves 6 as a first course.*

Buttered Scallops
See recipe above

Mussels

Of all shellfish, mussels are the least digestible. They should be chosen and prepared with great care and eaten on the day they are gathered or bought. They also can carry a poison in the 'liver' which is not destroyed by cooking. However, many hotels and restaurants now have mussels on their menus, the most popular type being Moules Marinières, which has been described as one of the world's greatest dishes.

Moules Marinières

To serve 4, you will probably need about 4 pints of mussels.

First, of course, the mussels must be selected, soaked, scrubbed and bearded under running water. Discard any with cracked or open shells. Place them in a buttered saucepan with ½ pint (300ml) white wine, a few chopped shallots, a bay leaf and *bouquet garni*. Put on the lid and stand over high heat, shaking the pan, for 3–5 minutes. This will cause the mussels to open their shells. They must then be picked over and any with unopened shells discarded, and any 'beards' taken out of opened mussels. Remove the empty top shells from the remainder, and put the 'inhabited' halves in a dish, or divided into individual dishes or soup plates. Strain over them the liquid they were cooked in. Sprinkle chopped parsley on top and serve at once.

Moules à la Poulette

In this dish, the mussels are prepared in just the same way as for Moules Marinières above, only the sauce being different. For this you mix ¼ pint (150ml) cream with 2 beaten egg yolks, the mussel liquid and the juice of a lemon. Cook over low heat until the sauce thickens and pour over the mussels.

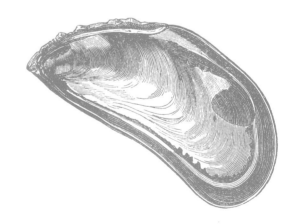

Grilled Salmon Cutlet
See page 19 for recipe

Prawns, Shrimps and Scampi

50 Very few people are able to go shrimping or gather prawns straight from the sea, but it is possible to obtain good fresh supplies already boiled, with or without their shells, from most fishmongers. Unshelled, they are usually sold by the pint, and shelled by weight, and are available fresh or frozen.

There are, of course, innumerable ways of using prawns. They are very good mixed with chopped celery and apple or with cold cooked flaked fish, but thick cream, seasoned and tinged with tomato purée, looks more attractive than mayonnaise.

The recipes given are for prawns and shrimps already shelled. They can also be bought potted and tinned, but the latter seem to have little flavour. It is rather hard luck on shrimps and prawns, freshly boiled in clear water (no additives), that they are also used as bait to catch salmon, although one angler confided in me that he'd only used two, because, absent-mindedly, he'd eaten the rest.

Shrimps are caught mainly off the north-west coast from Morecambe Bay to Solway Firth, but owing to an increasing demand, some are now imported.

Scampi, which come from the same family as the lobster, is another name for Dublin Bay Prawns. They have become increasingly popular in this country, sometimes as a starter to a meal, but more often, in larger quantities, as a main fish dish. In restaurants they are often rolled in egg and breadcrumbs, or batter, and fried in very hot oil. If you are fortunate enough to find them still in their shells, allow about 2lb (1kg) for 4 servings. Shelled, 1lb (450g) would be sufficient.

Prawn Cocktail

Prawn cocktail appears on most restaurant menus.   Here is my own version of this ever-popular favourite:

1lb (450g) shelled prawns
¼ pint (150ml) tomato ketchup
½ pint (300ml) cream
1 tablespoon freshly grated horseradish
few drops Tabasco, *or*
    2 teaspoons Worcestershire sauce
the juice of a lemon
1 lettuce, finely shredded
slices of lemon for garnish

Mix the tomato ketchup with the cream, freshly grated horseradish, the fiery Tabasco sauce (or a dessertspoon of Worcestershire sauce) and the lemon juice. Line serving glasses with the finely shredded lettuce, put about 2oz (50g) of shelled prawns in each, pour over the sauce and fix a thin slice of lemon on the edge of each glass. *Serves 8.*

Shrimps or chopped scampi can, of course, be substituted if no prawns are available.

If you are fortunate enough to obtain them another extremely good seafood cocktail can be made with crayfish (see Crayfish Cocktail, page 45).

Curried Prawns

I have hesitated about including curried prawns in my book because, although it is one of my favourite dishes, the very name evokes a painful memory.

On a summer day, a friend and I obeyed the order to 'go down to Kew in lilac time'. The gardens were magnificent, the sun shone, the fresh air raised an appetite and on the lunch-time menu was curried prawns, which were delicious. But venturing forth again, the sun had become torrid and by the time we had climbed an open-top bus, thirst had set in. From Kew Bridge we could see the Thames running softly, and again at Hammersmith. Crossing Hyde Park the Serpentine sparkled in the sun – it was 'Water, water everywhere, nor any drop to drink'. Now I know what dehydration means. Anyway, making sure liquid refreshment is plentiful, proceed as follows:

8oz (225g) peeled prawns
4oz (100g) shallots or spring onions
1 clove garlic
little oil for frying
2 tablespoons curry powder
3 tomatoes, skinned and chopped
1 tablespoon tomato purée
$\frac{1}{2}$ teaspoon cayenne pepper
1 tablespoon flour
$\frac{1}{2}$pt (300ml) stock
1 tablespoon mango chutney
squeeze of lemon juice
3 tablespoons double cream

Fry the chopped shallots or spring onions and a clove of crushed garlic in oil till soft. Stir in the curry powder, tomatoes, tomato purée and the cayenne pepper mixed with the flour. Gradually add the stock and cook over a low heat, stirring, till thick. Add the mango chutney and lemon juice. Simmer for a few minutes more, then add the peeled prawns. Lastly, stir in the double cream. *Serves 4.*

Some chefs use coconut juice instead of stock. Failing a fresh coconut, pour boiling water over 2 tablespoons of desiccated coconut, stir occasionally, strain and use the liquid.

This is usually served with boiled rice, but you can use cooked noodles or mashed potatoes for a change.

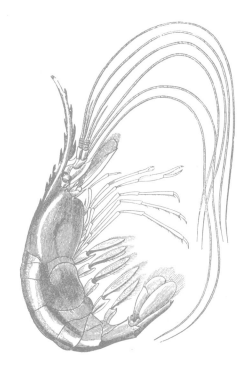

Prawn Pancakes

For the filling

12oz (350g) shelled prawns
1pt (600ml) Hollandaise Sauce (page 177)

For the pancakes

4oz (100g) plain flour
2 eggs
2 tablespoons oil
pinch of salt
¼ pint (150ml) milk

Beat – or blend – the pancake batter ingredients together in the order given above. Leave to stand for an hour. Make 12 thin pancakes. Spoon a little of the prawns onto the centre of each. Cover the filling with 2 tablespoons of Hollandaise Sauce and roll up the pancakes.

Arrange the pancakes in a lightly buttered shallow ovenproof dish. Mask them with the rest of the sauce and finish the dish in a hot oven (425°F, 210°C, gas mark 7) for about 10 minutes, or under the grill. *Serves 6.*

Tennessee Pilaff

2 cups peeled shrimps
1 cup long grain rice
4 rashers bacon
2oz (50g) butter
½ cup celery, finely chopped
½ cup green pepper, finely chopped
salt and pepper
few drops Worcestershire sauce

Cook the rice in the usual way and keep warm. Fry the bacon till crisp. Remove from pan, augment the bacon fat with the butter and sauté the celery and green pepper for a few minutes. Season with salt, pepper and a few drops of Worcestershire sauce. Add the peeled shrimps, stir in the boiled rice, mix well and finally add the bacon, crumbled. *Serves 6.*

Prawns or scampi can be substituted for the shrimps.

Vermont Shrimps

1lb (450g) cooked peeled shrimps
2oz (50g) butter
1 cup cider vinegar
2 eggs, separated

Melt the butter in the top of a double boiler, add the vinegar and cooked peeled shrimps and cook for 5 minutes. Beat the 2 egg yolks. To prevent curdling, take a little of the hot liquor from the pan and gradually add to the eggs, then mix all together. Heat up until smooth, but do not allow to boil. Cool, then fold in the whipped egg whites. Serve in glasses on a bed of shredded lettuce leaves and dusted with paprika. *Serves 4.*

Tomatoes Stuffed with Shrimps

6 large tomatoes
6oz (150g) peeled shrimps
1 small onion, chopped
1 teaspoon chopped parsley
salt and pepper
2 tablespoons mayonnaise
1 tablespoon tomato ketchup
few drops Worcestershire sauce

Slice the tops off the tomatoes and scoop out and discard the seeds. Mix together the peeled shrimps, chopped onion, chopped parsley, salt and pepper. Add the mayonnaise, tomato ketchup and a few drops of Worcestershire sauce. Mix well and fill the hollowed-out tomatoes. Serve with thin slices of buttered brown bread. *Serves 6.*

Scampi Provençale

1lb (450g) peeled scampi
1 medium onion, chopped
1 clove garlic, crushed
oil or butter for frying
1 glass dry white wine
6 medium tomatoes, peeled and sliced
6 large mushrooms, sliced

Fry the onion and crushed clove of garlic in oil or butter for a few minutes, add the glass of dry white wine, the tomatoes and mushrooms, salt and pepper and finally the peeled scampi. You could use a tin of tomatoes, if more convenient, and omit the mushrooms. Serve in a ring of boiled rice. *Serves 4.*

Clam Chowder

Clams. These molluscs, originally American and perennially associated with that country, are in fact widely available on the Atlantic coast of France and now being cultivated in Britain. Sold in the shell, like oysters, they are also opened and eaten like them – raw, with lemon juice and a little cayenne. They are in season all the year round, but at their best in the autumn.

This is, of course, all-American, and we can't often make it fresh from the sea, as our friends do. But, failing these, you can obtain a tin of clams and with this a good imitation is possible.

1 tin of clams
3–4 rashers fat bacon
1 medium onion, minced
1 green pepper, chopped
a little oil for frying
black pepper
½pt (300ml) *béchamel* sauce (page 172)

Fry the rashers of fat bacon, cut into small pieces, till crisp and put aside. Fry the onion and green pepper in the bacon fat, adding a little oil if necessary, then the clams complete with liquor and some black pepper. Simmer for 30 minutes, add the bacon crisps and a cup of white sauce. Heat up and serve. *Serves 4.*

4

Carp and Pike

But now the sport is marde and
wott ye why?
Fishes decrease and fishers multiply!

Thomas Bastard, 1598

Carp

The carp originated in southern Asia. It was introduced into Europe in Roman times and into Britain, it is said, in 1514.

Perhaps more on the Continent than in Britain, the flesh is highly esteemed for both texture and flavour, and carp are bred in ponds, some extending to thousands of acres, where the water is actually 'manured' to encourage prolific growth of plants, etc., on which the fish feed. They are then moved, like trout, to tanks where they are kept ready for the market. But in our own country, in medieval times, the monks, who had well-appointed kitchens, maintained large ponds in which to breed carp, and 'ice-houses' sunk in the abbey grounds, ensuring that nice fresh fish would be available for the Friday fast, thereby conforming to the rules of the Catholic church. And woe betide any friar who strayed from that particular path of righteousness, like Claude Guillan who, in 1629, was beheaded at St Claude for eating a morsel of horseflesh on a 'Fishday'. If Claude had been less ingenuous and more ingenious, he might have learned from that unscrupulous character, Chicot (in one of Alexandre Dumas's books), who, having produced a fine fat capon, persuaded guileless Gorenflot to baptize it (in the name of Bacchus, Momus and Comus), naming it 'Carp', after which it was cooked as a carp, with butter and shallots, and served on hot toast.

Some time ago, I was astounded to read, in an article by an angling journalist, a diatribe against carp. 'A fish, yes,' he wrote, 'food, never.' And he went on: 'Even smothered in the best of sauces, nothing can disguise the fact that the basic flesh has the consistency of cotton wool, liberally reinforced with needles. Nothing can remove the underlying taint of stagnant moat.' Even more surprising was the fact that the writer had caught his carp, which was cooked for him, in that land of *haute cuisine*, France.

However, it was on a Friday when he caught another and, seeing his landlady hurrying towards him, he tried frantically to throw it back. But she had only hastened to tell him that the parish priest had pronounced that she could cook a fine fat duck for dinner, since being aquatic, it could be classed with fish. What, by the way, is the difference between aquatic and amphibious? What is the difference between abstinence and fasting? And if that angler did eat that carp he loathed, shouldn't that count for merit?

Anyhow some of the *maigre* meals of the past must have made Lucifer laugh. In 1845, there was a rumour that the Pope was coming on a visit to England, and the question arose as to how he was to be entertained, especially on the Friday, the day of penance and fasting.

Famous chefs submitted menus and the one finally chosen for the 'fast' day was:

Hors-d'œuvres

Les huitres.   Les whitebait.
Les laitances de maquereaux frites.
Le curry de homards. Les goujons frites.
Les bandelettes de saumon fumé.
Les moules au gratin.

Potages

A la tortue claire.
Les perches en souchet.
Les filets de soles à la Bagration.

Relevés

Le saumon à la régence.
L'esturgeon à la royale.
Le turbot à la Parisienne.
Le brochet à la Chambord.
Le matelots de carpe et d'anguille au
vin de bourgogne.
Les lamproies à la Beauchamp.
Le vol-au-vent de morue.
Les filets de truites au velouté.
d'écrevisses.
Le pâté de filets de merlans.
Les filets de rougets à la Beaufort.

Entremets ·

Les écrevisses en buisson.
Les prawns en buisson.
La mayonnaise de thon marine.

And to round it off, various elaborate desserts made with *pêches, poires, fraises, ananas,* oranges and apples.

Surely the last vast fast.

Way back in 1466, the Archbishop of York gave a feast at which 'a great number of pike were dressed' and in 1487 a feast was given at Whitehall at which 'Carpe in Foile' and 'Pike in Latymer Sawce' were included in the menu. It was in that period that carp was sometimes called the kissing fish, because when they suck insects off the undersides of leaves, they make a noise like human (smacking wet) kisses.

The Protestants of Elizabeth I's reign protested against fasting and fish on Friday, but those in power tried to keep the custom going, both to encourage the sea-fishing industry and to check the consumption of meat, which encouraged the conversion of arable land into pasture.

A century ago, the carp was described as 'by far the best fish for artificial management, especially that variety known as the Prussian carp, which feed on earth-worms and aquatic insects and require little artificial food during the Winter months, whilst in Summer they will consume various waste products'.

While trout farming is nowadays the most rewarding, there have been attempts in recent years to breed carp also. It was about 1974 that I was given the address of Newhay Fisheries, near Selby in Yorkshire, where pedigree carp imported from Bavaria and called *Dinkel-bühler* were bred in low-lying land bordering the river Ouse. I don't know if it is still in existence. There is also, I'm told, a carp farm at North Sarle in Lincolnshire.

Carp grow to a vast size, compared to the average freshwater fish; the largest landed in England (by Richard Walker) weighed 44lb (20kg) and was kept in the London Zoo Aquarium for some years before it died.

Because of its size and lack of the favour of fine flavour, the carp, except in the case of very small specimens, is usually best cleaned, cut up and cooked in fillets. Where there is soft roe, this should be used separately as a savoury (see Curé's Omelette, page 61).

Stuffed Carp

1 large carp
1oz (25g) butter

For the stuffing
1 onion, sliced
4oz (100g) mushrooms, sliced
2 eggs
1½oz (40g) softened butter
2oz (50g) fresh breadcrumbs
salt and pepper

If you have a large carp which you would like to present whole, then it must be stuffed and baked. Clean it very thoroughly, leaving the head on. To make the stuffing, fry the sliced onion in a little of the butter till transparent, add the sliced mushrooms and a little water. Cook for 5 minutes. Separate the 2 eggs, beat the yolks with the rest of the softened butter and the breadcrumbs. Season with salt and pepper. Add this to the mushrooms. Whisk the egg whites and fold in to the mixture. Stuff the carp, closing the sides with small skewers. Grease a baking dish, dot the fish with butter, cover with foil and bake in a preheated moderate oven (350°F, 180°C, gas mark 4), basting occasionally for about 30 minutes. Remove foil for last 10 minutes.

Carp Cardinal

For small carp, clean carefully and put in a fireproof dish. Slice 2 onions and 2 peeled apples, add a pinch each of sage, marjoram and tarragon, salt and pepper and mix with ¼ pint (150ml) of cider vinegar. Spread this over the fish, cover and cook in a moderate oven (350°F, 180°C, gas mark 4) for 30 minutes.

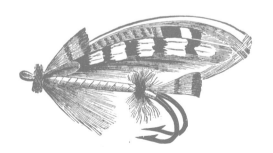

Baked Carp

Clean and scale a medium-sized carp, leaving on the head and tail, and curl round in a heat-proof dish. Mix 3 tablespoons olive oil, 1 tablespoon each of Worcestershire sauce, lemon juice, chopped parsley and onion. Add salt, black pepper and cayenne pepper. Pour this over the fish and let it marinate for about 2 hours, basting at intervals. Cover and bake in a slow oven (325°F, 160°C, gas mark 3) for an hour. Serve on a hot dish with the juices and a white sauce (page 172) to which a few chopped gherkins have been added.

A slightly more elaborate way of baking carp is to slice and cook in butter, tomatoes, onions, a clove of garlic, red pepper and a few slices of potato, seasoned with salt and pepper. When soft, lay on the carp, dusted inside and out with salt and paprika. Pour over some cream and use this for basting occasionally for the 30 to 40 minutes needed. Add a cup of shrimps before serving.

Izaak Walton's Way

Looking at the beautiful stained-glass window in Winchester Cathedral, dedicated to Izaak Walton, described on a memorial stone there as the 'Patriarch of Anglers', who would think he was so singularly unfeeling about both his bait and his bite? Telling his readers to impale a live frog on the hook, he says 'use him as though you loved him, that he may live the longer'.

Likewise in his recipes, such as the following one for carp:

Take a carp, alive if possible, scour him with water and salt but scale him not. Open him and put him with his blood and liver into a pot; then take marjoram, thyme and parsley of each a handful and a sprig of rosemary, put them in your carp with four or five whole onions, twenty oysters and three anchovies. Pour upon your carp as much claret wine as will cover him and season with salt, cloves, mace and the rinds of oranges and lemons. Cover and set on a quick fire till it be sufficiently boiled. Then take out the carp, lay it with the broth into the dish and pour upon him a quarter of a pound of the best fresh butter, melted and beaten with half-a-dozen spoonsful of the broth, the yolks of two or three eggs and some of the herbs shred, garnish your dish with lemons and so serve it up. And much good do you!

Samuel Pepys was also evidently appreciative of the carp as culinary provender. In his famous diary he writes: 'At noon come my good guests – I had a pretty dinner for them, viz., a brace of stewed carps, six roasted chickens and a jowl of salmon, hot, for the first course; very merry all the afternoon talking and singing and piping upon the flageolette.'

Spiced Baked Carp

From Missouri comes this simple recipe for baked carp.

Skin the carp and cut into 2-inch (5cm) pieces, put in an oiled earthenware dish, sprinkle with salt and pepper, cover with a generous handful of whole, mixed spices, and a cupful of vinegar, and bake in a moderate oven (350°F, 180°C, gas mark 4) for an hour. And the cook adds, 'that oughta tame them bones down to where they don't bother'.

Carp Portugaise

6 small carp
1oz (25g) butter

For the stuffing

1 cup breadcrumbs
1 teaspoon shredded suet
1 tablespoon onion, minced
1 tablespoon celery, minced
1 tablespoon grated cheese
1 teaspoon anchovy essence
1 egg, beaten

OR

1 cup packet thyme and parsley stuffing mix
1 egg, beaten
2 tablespoons Worcestershire sauce

Clean and fillet the carp. Mix together the stuffing ingredients, binding them with the beaten egg. (Where time is limited, a good substitute can be made with a packet of thyme and parsley stuffing mixture made up as directed, to which you add a beaten egg and 2 tablespoons of Worcestershire sauce.)

Spread this over each fillet, then roll up and secure with a small skewer. Pack into a casserole, dot with butter, cover and bake in a moderate oven (350°F, 180°C, gas mark 4) for half an hour. A sauce is hardly needed, but a simple white sauce (page 171), heated with 2oz (50g) grated cheese and a pinch of cayenne, adds interest and a few lemon slices make a good garnish. *Serves 6.*

Carp à Fleuve

The French are fond of mixed fish dishes (such as Bouillabaisse) and there is no reason why different fish should not be amalgamated most successfully. Along the banks of the Seine, for example, carp, tench and eels are often cooked together. This recipe should be suitable for whatever fish you may have.

First, remove the heads and clean the fish; should your 'catch' include eels, skin them (see page 92). Cut all the fish in thick slices and roll in seasoned flour. Allow 2 medium-sized onions for each 1lb (450g) of fish and fry these in butter. When soft, add a tablespoon of flour mixed into 2oz (50g) butter and stir well. Pour in red *vin ordinaire*, a crushed clove of garlic, thyme, parsley and bay leaf, salt and pepper.

Bring to the boil and simmer a few minutes, then put in the fish and cook for 25 minutes. Serve with fried or toasted bread.

The fish and methods differ from one area to another, some preferring white wine, others using beaten egg yolks to thicken the sauce. Sometimes the herbs are tied together and removed before completion, some fry the bread in olive oil and rub with garlic and, for special occasions, brandy is poured on the fish and set alight.

George I once complained – and with some reason – that while on one day he was told that St James's Park was his park, yet that 'the next day Lord Chetwynd [Ranger of the park] sent me a brace of carp out of my water and I was told I must give five guineas to his man for bringing my own carp out of my own canal, in my own park' (James Saunders, 1723).

Florentine Fillets

This is equally suitable for carp or pike fillets.

6 carp or pike fillets
spinach
salt and pepper
a pinch of dill
cayenne pepper
1pt (600ml) *béchamel* sauce (page 172)
4oz (100g) grated cheese, plus 1 tablespoon
celery salt
1 tablespoon breadcrumbs
1oz (25g) butter

Cook sufficient spinach to cover a shallow baking dish (about 3lb (1½kg) should be enough for 6 servings). Lay the fillets of fish on this, season with salt and pepper and a pinch each of dill and cayenne pepper.

Heat the *béchamel* sauce, and stir in the grated cheese and a little celery salt. Pour over the fish. Mix the extra tablespoon of grated cheese with the breadcrumbs, sprinkle over the sauce and dot with the butter. Bake for 25 minutes in a fairly hot oven (400°F, 200°C, gas mark 6).

As an alternative put lemon slices between the fish in the baking dish. Cover with a layer of mushrooms and a little stock. Cover and cook for 30 minutes. Discard the lemon before serving. Use the mushrooms as above instead of cheese. *Serves 6.*

Curé's Omlette

4oz (100g) carp roe, chopped
a little butter
1 small shallot, finely chopped
4oz (100g) cooked carp, flaked
salt and pepper
4 eggs, well beaten

If your carp has a soft roe, pour boiling water over it, drain, cool and leave till next day. Next, melt a little butter in an omelette pan and cook the finely chopped shallot, add the cooked carp, stir and then put in the chopped roe. Season with salt and pepper and pour over the well-beaten eggs. Cook till just set – not too long as the roe should stay soft. Put a dab of *maître d'hôtel* butter (page 177) on top and serve immediately. (And your guests wouldn't know the difference if you used tinned herring roes.) *Serves 2.*

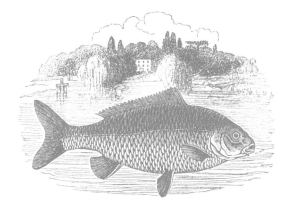

62 And here I would mention H. T. Shering-ham's advice to would-be carp catchers. He wrote, 'It is certain that good luck is the most vital part of the equipment of him who would seek to slay big carp. Avoid old women who squint, throw salt over your left shoulder, touch wood, be on friendly terms with black cats.'

> *And when magpies pass, tradition states,*
> *One may avert the evil fates*
> *By swiftly turning from the sight*
> *And smartly spitting to the right.*

These things are important in carp fishing, but all anglers seem to have superstitions, although they vary widely. Some refer to specific fish while others affect the day's sport generally. That exceptionally wise angler, Norman Hill, lists a whole range of auguries. A magpie shares equally with a nun as a bad omen, although a black cat or a bullfinch will offset the threat.

My son Richard claims that magpies only desire to be treated with the courtesy to which all creatures are entitled. If he sees one, he raises his hat and says, 'Good morning, Mr Magpie' (lacking a hat, he genuflects!). His angling friend, David Myers, now follows the same procedure, but sceptical Pete Thomas scorns such notions. However, when the three were on their way to the trout fishery at Damerham, no fewer than seven magpies flew across their path. Richard and David said, 'Good morning, Mr Magpie' (and raised hats) seven times. Pete gave the birds a Harvey Smith salute with a derisory remark. But at the end of the day, Richard and David had each four fine fat trout and Pete's only catch was a small, blackish, feeble specimen. Richard also claims that success is assured if one happens on a Salvation Army band and stops to give a donation. I remember one occasion when, in a narrow street, we held up a whole line of traffic to enable him to alight and cross the road to bestow his offering.

Pike

The Pike fell tyrant of the liquid plain
With rav'nous waste devours his fellow-train.

Thomas Best, 1779

The pike has a long body, flat jaw, a big mouth stretching to its eyes and strong sharp teeth. It is ferocious, ravenous and rapacious, a murderous marauder, a squalid scavenger; it has an insatiable appetite and is a callous cannibal. There is a legend that the only other fishes which can feel safe from a pike are the perch and the tench, because even that callous creature is aware of the array of sharp points on the back of the perch, while the tench is considered to have healing properties and even a pike is loath to attack the family doctor. But, in fact, pike willingly eat both perch and tench.

It is written in *The Treatyse of Fysshynge* (Dame Juliana Berners, 1496) that 'The pike is a good fysshe; but for he devouryth so many of his owne kind as of other, I love hym the lesse'. Yet, in medieval times, in central Europe, there was a superstition that the pike's head was made from a cross, three nails and a sword, because it was the only fish that had no feeling and watched the Crucifixion.

But earlier on, in the story of Tobias, we are told that 'a fish leaped out of the river and would have devoured him'. I don't know anything about the fish in Iran or what swims in the Tigris, but I have always visualized that fish as an outsize pike. However, you remember that Tobias was accompanied by his guardian angel Azarias, which is probably why Tobias just 'laid hold of the fish and drew it to land and when he had taken out the heart, liver and gall (which he carefully preserved) they roasted the fish and they did eat it'. A clear case of the biter bit and 'waste

not, want not'. Because, in case you've forgotten the rest of the story, the travellers arrived at their destination, where Tobias promptly fell in love with his cousin Sara, only to be warned that she had already been married seven times, although the poor young husbands, each and every one, had been frightened to death by a wicked devil, ere ever he had reached the marriage chamber.

But Tobias was not to be deterred and the marriage feast went ahead, with the burning of incense, aromatic herbs and spices, which naturally reminded Tobias of that fish's giblets, by now somewhat redolent. He also remembered the advice given him by Azarias and quickly gathered up handfuls of sandalwood herbal ashes and shewbread, took them to his room, put the heart and liver on them and set it all alight. Sure enough, that old devil came along with his fell designs, but it befell, when he smelt that smell, that he let out a yell of 'No spell! Farewell!' and went like a bat to Hell! And Tobias murmured, 'Well! Well! Tis a consummation devoutly to be wished,' and he returned to the feast and claimed his bride. Next day they set out for home, without any pause for angling.

I should have mentioned, for the uninitiated, that the father of Tobias had, rather shortsightedly, slept by a wall where sparrows nested and, opening his eyes at an inopportune moment, he received droppings which left a whiteness in them, making him blind. But Tobias once more remembered his friend's advice and, as his father ran, stumbling to meet him, he smeared that old pike's gall on his father's eyes, which naturally made them smart more than somewhat and he rubbed them so hard that not only did he remove the gall, but the whiteness 'pilled away' also and he could see his son. Which shows how useful a guardian angel can be, even when catching or cooking fish.

Perhaps because of the pike's sanguinary character, Izaak Walton enjoyed pitting his skill and wits against the fish's natural cunning. Indeed he spent so many hours angling for pike that Leigh Hunt in *The Indicator and Companion* said, 'He looks like a pike, dressed in broadcloth instead of butter.' Izaak also gives a recipe, evidently entrusted to him by someone else, for cooking pike. The ingredients are much the same as for carp, except that the fish is stuffed up, sewn up, tied up, roasted on a spit and basted with claret wine. He adds a footnote: 'This dish of meat is too good for any but anglers or very honest men; and I trust you will prove both and therefore I have trusted you with this secret.'

My first memory of a pike was when my father, whose farm was beside a river, saw one of the brutes seize and swallow a small dab-chick. Whereupon my father vowed vengeance. He was no angler, but he fixed up some crude tackle – a clothes prop, a length of cord, and a small meat hook, on which was impaled a slab of raw meat – and he landed that pike, which ended up as food for the fowl.

My last sight of a pike was when my son, who had repeatedly been told by a German friend living with me how good the fish is to eat, brought along two he had caught and laid them reverently on the kitchen floor. One weighed 17lb (8kg) and the other 20lb (9kg). When I saw them, looking like malevolent crocodiles and I knew that Dick had his tongue in his cheek and a twinkle in his eye, I gave him prompt marching orders and told him to take his captives with him.

In France the pike is highly regarded as food and is expensive to buy, although Escoffier is said to have used pike only in the preparation of his celebrated forcemeat and quenelles. In Great Britain it is seldom, if ever, for sale, although it has been stated that in the thirteenth century, the price was double that of salmon and it was in great demand.

The Rev. James Woodforde (author of *The Diary of a Country Parson*) was inordinately proud of his big pike. He wrote:

The largest Fish we caught was a Pike which was a yard long and weighted upwards of thirteen pounds. Next day, I gave my Company for dinner my great Pike which was rosted and a Pudding in his Belly, some boiled Trout, Perch and Tench, Eel and Gudgeon fryed. All my Company were quite astonished at the sight of the great Pike. Was obliged to lay him on two of the largest dishes . . . laid on part of the Kitchen Window shutters covered with a cloth. I never saw a nobler Fish at any table, it was very well cooked and tho' so large was declared by all the Company to be prodigious fine eating, being so moist.

Although the flesh is coarse and dry, with the help of herbs, spices and good sauces, pike can be made very palatable. The smaller pike – up to 3lb (1½kg) – are usually called Jack, but for cooking, large pike are considered better. A 3lb (1½kg) fish will yield six servings.

Mrs Beeton has given instructions for baking, boiling and frying pike, which I repeat opposite. In each case the fish must first be thoroughly cleaned and scaled, the fins and gills removed, and any roe discarded.

Mursley Trout
See page 28 for recipe

Baked Pike

Make a forcemeat with 4 tablespoons chopped suet, 1 teaspoon chopped parsley, 1 egg, the grated rind of a lemon, a pinch of salt, pepper and nutmeg. Mix all together, stuff the pike, then brush it over with beaten egg, cover with fried breadcrumbs and dot with butter. Bake in a slow oven (325°F, 160°C, gas mark 3) for 40–45 minutes and serve with Hollandaise sauce (page 177).

Boiled Pike

Heat a large pan of water to which cloves, a bouquet garni, vinegar and salt have been added, put in the stuffed fish and simmer gently for 25–30 minutes for a 4lb (2kg) fish.

As this is a very plain dish, it would be a good idea to accompany it with a characterful sauce. Two good ones to try would be anchovy or any piquant sauce (see sauce section).

Fried Pike

For larger fish, clean and scale as usual, cut into slices (not too thick), soak for a time in cold water (which firms them), dry, rub lightly with seasoned flour, then coat with egg and breadcrumbs and fry in hot fat. Sprinkle with lemon juice.

For a change, you can boil the pike (as directed by Mrs Beeton), then, when well cooked, remove skin and bones, put some melted butter in a fireproof dish, put in the fish, sprinkle with salt and a little cayenne pepper and pour over a little more melted butter. Cover with a layer of sliced tomatoes and onions, then wrap in foil and bake in a fairly hot oven (400°F, 200°C, gas mark 6) for 10–15 minutes. (You can use canned tomatoes, draining off the liquid to serve, with a dash of Worcestershire sauce, as cocktails.)

Grayling Gaillard
See page 81 for recipe

Le Brochet de Vouvray

This is one of the best French ways of dealing with pike.

1 fine pike, weighing about 3lb (1½kg)
glass of white wine
1 carrot, sliced
1 onion, sliced
bouquet garni
salt
a few peppercorns

For the sauce

6 shallots, finely chopped
½pt (300ml) dry white wine
4oz (100g) butter
2 tablespoons cream

Put the glass of white wine in a large pan with 1 pint (600ml) of water, the carrot and onion, a *bouquet garni*, salt and peppercorns. Cook for about 20 minutes, then leave it to cool. Put in the fish, bring to the boil, and cook for another 25 minutes.

While all this cooking is going on, make the special sauce:

Put the shallots into a pan with the white wine and ¼ pint (150ml) of the liquor in which the fish is cooking. Let this boil gently until reduced to half, then take off the direct heat and put in the top of a double boiler, or pan, over hot water. Gradually add the butter and 2 tablespoons of cream. When frothy, serve with the fish. *Serves 6.*

Escoffier's Brochet Lyonnaise

½lb (225g) pike meat
4oz (100g) breadcrumbs
a little milk
4oz (100g) softened butter
2 eggs, beaten
salt and pepper
a little flour

Purée the pike meat. Soak the white breadcrumbs in milk, then squeeze tightly so you have a thick bread paste. Mix this with the softened butter and the fish purée. Add the beaten eggs, salt and pepper, roll into thin sausage shapes about 2 inches long on a floured board, and poach the dumplings in gently boiling salted water for about 10 minutes. *Serves 4.*

Pike Vermont

1 pike
1 tablespoon minced onion
1 teaspoon dry mustard
pinch each of marjoram, oregano, paprika
    and freshly ground black pepper
½pt (300ml) dry white wine
1 lemon

Clean the pike and remove the backbone. Lay the fillets in a buttered baking dish. Mix together the minced onion, dry mustard, marjoram, oregano, paprika and black pepper in the white wine. Add the juice of the lemon and spoon this over the fish. Bake, uncovered, in a hot oven (425°F, 220°C, gas mark 7) for 20–25 minutes. Garnish with slivers of lemon peel. *Serves 6.*

Collared Pike

1 pike, divided into 4 fillets
forcemeat
2 rashers lean bacon
2 tablespoons finely chopped shallot
2 tablespoons parsley
½lb (225g) tomatoes
2 medium apples
2 teaspoons Worcestershire sauce
salt and pepper

A very savoury dish can be made by using the pike in this way. On each of the fillets, spread some well-flavoured forcemeat (I suggest you try that given in Mrs Beeton's recipe for Baked Pike, page 65), roll up and wrap a rasher of bacon round each. Lay these close together in a well-greased fireproof dish. Sprinkle over them the chopped shallot and parsley. Peel and slice the tomatoes and apples. Mix these together and arrange in a layer over the fish. Add 2 teaspoons of Worcestershire sauce, salt and pepper, cover with well-oiled foil and bake for 25 minutes in a moderate oven (350°F, 180°C, gas mark 4), removing the foil 5 minutes before the end of the cooking time. *Serves 4.*

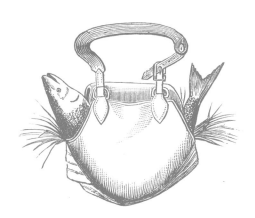

Pike Casserole

1 large pike, filleted
1 green pepper, chopped
1 onion, minced
1 tablespoon Dijon mustard
1 teaspoon Worcestershire sauce
few drops Tabasco sauce
the juice of 2 lemons
4oz (100g) melted butter
6oz (175g) white breadcrumbs
2 tablespoons grated cheese

Clean and fillet the pike. Mix together the chopped green pepper and minced onion, Dijon mustard, Worcestershire sauce, Tabasco sauce and the lemon juice. Stir in the melted butter and breadcrumbs. Put half of this in a casserole, lay on the pike fillets, cover with the rest of the mixture and bake for 25–30 minutes in a moderate oven (350°F, 180°C, gas mark 4). Sprinkle over the grated cheese and return to the oven, or put under the grill for a few minutes, to brown. *Serves 6.*

Many fishermen who know Fred J. Taylor as an angling expert and a much-travelled author and journalist are well aware that he is also a superb cook. I look back to an outstanding dinner at my home, when Fred cooked the Windermere char contributed by Fred Buller, and a large turbot brought by Leslie Moncrieff. He also made superb game pies with the offerings of our wild-fowler friends, who tried to convince Maurice Wiggin that the contents included hedgehog (which however did not deter Maurice from taking a second helping). During his travels across America, Fred acquired the recipe overleaf from Mrs Dorothy Vasconcellos of Minnesota and it has become a favourite among his fishing companions.

Pike Fingers à la Vasconcellos

1 4–5lb (2–2½kg) pike
Rice Crispies
plain potato crisps
melted butter

Fillet, skin and cut the pike into 'fish finger' sized pieces. Roll out into crumbs equal quantities of Rice Crispies and plain potato crisps. Dip the fish fingers into *very hot* melted butter and roll them in the crumbs. Lay them in a non-stick baking dish and bake in a hot oven (425°F, 220°C, gas mark 7) for 10–15 minutes. *Do not* overbake. *Do not* use warm or cooling butter as this makes fish greasy. Any breakfast cereal (not sweetened) will do, but Rice Crispies seem to be best. These fingers are delicious cold next day with salad. The recipe works also with trout and all non-oily kinds of fish. *Serves 8–10.*

Maybe you have already heard the story of the two Yorkshiremen who went fishing. After some time of fruitless endeavour, one of them caught and hauled out a monster pike. After a few minutes of amazed admiration, he detached it from the hook and hurled it back into the water. 'Whatever didst tha do that for?' asked his friend. 'It wer too big,' he said, 'nobody wud ever a' believed I'd caught it.'

Patrick Chalmers, in his delightful book, *At the Tail of the Weir*, writes:

Anyone can cook a salmon or a trout and make a feast of it, but let the epicure beware of prejudice. I will tell you a little memory of my own to illustrate the folly of prejudging any case before it is tried:

There was a salmon angler whose Silver Doctor was taken by a pike as sometimes happens. The pike was gaffed and went up to the house.

'What,' asked the lady, 'shall I do with the pike?'

'Pitch it away,' replied her lord.

'Pitch it away,' echoed Lieutenant-General Sir Currie Rice, 'pitch it away at once, my dear lady, pike is poison.'

But the lady was not one to pitch away any of heaven's mercies. Next evening the menu card announced Cold Mayonnaise of Turbot. And a lovely-looking mayonnaise it was that the butler handed, golden with the sieved yolks of eggs and crisp with green lettuce.

Sir Currie has two goes at it and is looking hopefully over his shoulder to see if Crichton is to hand it a third time, while the master of the house, scraping his platter, exclaims at the excellence of the turbot and says that one gets devilish tired of salmon.

And, of course, it was the boned pike they ate so gladly.

5
Smaller Freshwater Fish

I love any discourse of rivers and fish and
fishing

Izaak Walton

Some anglers are interested only in salmon, trout and sea-trout, and any other fish which may be accidentally hooked are thrown back into the water or – so I have read – hurled unceremoniously up the bank and there left to expire. Keen Scottish game fishermen claim that the coarse fish take too much out of the rivers, not only their usual food but, in the case of pike and even perch, also the salmon and trout fry.

Indeed, I remember an article by a renowned angling writer who reported that he was admonished by a water bailiff for emptying his keepnet of beautiful two-pounder roach back into a swim. 'You're not supposed to do that,' the bailiff said, 'they're coarse fish, you're supposed to kill 'em.' And he stamped off, none too pleased as the last few were wriggling back to freedom.

However, English anglers genuinely dislike killing fish but enjoy fishing Scottish lochs or rivers for pike, perch and roach. Two famous angling authors have stated, 'Most coarse anglers return their catch alive – they are missing little.' Which is why, perhaps, that consummate *artiste*, Frankie Vaughan, a dedicated angler, never, apparently, takes his fish home. Asked for his favourite fish dish, he plumped for Baked Cod Casserole. In 1974 however, he selected Herrings in Oatmeal (fried), so he evidently puts catching the cooking before cooking the catch.

Having in mind the cost of living, it is worth while making the best and the most of edible fish, even if they are not in the epicure class. It is surprising what can be produced with a few fish and the exercise of a little ingenuity. That eighteenth-century cleric and undoubted epicure, James Woodforde, in his book *The Diary of a Country Parson*, mentions eating tench, roach, chub, dace and (frequently) pike.

Barbel

Although anglers respect the barbel as one of the hardest fish to catch, its flesh is rather coarse and considered by some as scarcely worth cooking (the roe is alleged to be poisonous). Nevertheless, *The Treatyse of Fysshynge* tells us that 'the barbel is a swete fysshe'. In Spain and in some parts of France it is eaten as a matter of course.

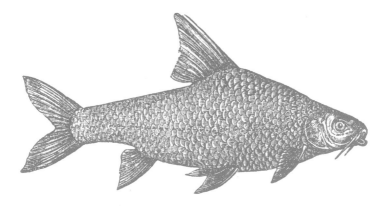

Poached Barbel

The fish must first be cleaned and soaked in salt water, then rinsed and put again into clean water, to which 1 cup of vinegar has been added.

Make a *court bouillon* by cooking some chopped onions, carrots and celery with mixed herbs, including mace, in a good stock until the vegetables are soft, season with salt and pepper then lay the fish in, bring to the boil, add 2 anchovies, turn the heat down and simmer gently for 30 minutes. Remove the fish to a warmed dish, garnish with chopped parsley and serve hot with horseradish and cream or caper sauce, or cold with vinaigrette or mayonnaise (see sauces section for recipes).

Baked Barbel

Prepare the fish as for poaching (see previous recipe), dry and stuff with breadcrumbs, chopped mushrooms and hard-boiled egg, season, and bind with a little milk. Lay in a fireproof dish, scatter breadcrumbs on top, pour over $\frac{1}{4}$ pint (150ml) red wine, dot with butter, cover and bake in a moderate oven (350°F, 180°C, gas mark 4) for about 25 minutes.

Bream

The bream is a flat fish, rather dry, very bony and insipid, but it can be made into quite a good dish.

If they are small, one of the simplest and most effective ways of cooking bream is to roll them in oatmeal, fry them crisply in bacon fat, and serve them with lemon wedges, brown bread and butter.

To prepare bream for cooking, remove head and fins but not the scales, clean well, rub over with salt and wash again.

Boiled Bream

Clean the bream, put in a pan and cover with hot water, add salt and pepper, bring to the boil and then simmer for about 45 minutes. Garnish with slices of lemon and serve with mustard sauce (page 173).

Baked Bream

The fish can be cooked whole, wrapped in oiled foil and baked in a moderate oven (350°F, 180°C, gas mark 4) for about 30–40 minutes. Alternatively, it can be stuffed with forcemeat – a mixture of breadcrumbs, suet, finely chopped anchovy, salt, pepper and a pinch of mace, bound with a beaten egg.

Baked Fillets of Bream with Bacon

2lb (1kg) bream fillets
butter
salt and pepper
a little milk
6 rashers lean, back bacon
flour

Butter a large ovenproof dish. Dip the bream fillets in seasoned flour and lay them in the dish. Pour over a little milk, lay the rashers on top, place the dish in a hot oven (450°F, 200°C, gas mark 6) for 20–25 minutes. *Serves 4.*

Bream Baked with Oysters and Lemon

If the fish are small enough to serve one to each guest, put an oyster and a squeeze of lemon into the cavity. When oysters are not available use mushrooms. Put the whole fish side by side in a dish, cover each with a long slice of streaky bacon and cook in a moderate oven (350°F, 180°C, gas mark 4) for 30 minutes.

Bream Bakemeat

This recipe was given me by an Australian friend, and I think it is intended for sea-bream. However, it is well worth trying with our freshwater fish.

2–3 bream
butter for frying
4oz (100g) onion, chopped
4oz (100g) mushrooms, chopped
salt
cayenne pepper
12oz (350g) shortcrust pastry

The bream must first be well cleaned, filleted and fried in butter. Set aside. In the same pan fry the chopped onions and mushrooms for a few minutes. Season with salt and cayenne pepper. Roll out the shortcrust pastry into a rectangle. Put half on a flat baking sheet and spread over it half the onion and mushroom mixture. Lay the bream fillets on this, then the rest of the onion and mushroom mixture. Finally, cover with the rest of the pastry. Moisten the edges with a little cold water, press together to seal and bake in a moderate oven (350°F, 180°C, gas mark 4) for 25 minutes. *Serves 6.*

Bream Plaki

3 bream
salt and freshly ground black pepper
1 lemon
a little olive oil
1 onion, minced
1 clove garlic, crushed
1lb (450g) tomatoes, skinned and chopped *or*
    6oz (150g) grated cheese
2 tablespoons minced parsley
1 teaspoon coriander powder
¼pt (150ml) white wine

Clean and scale the fish and put whole in a well-greased baking dish. Sprinkle with salt, black pepper and the juice of the lemon. Fry the minced onion and crushed clove of garlic in olive oil until soft; stir in the skinned and chopped tomatoes, add the minced parsley, coriander powder and white wine. Cook till well blended, pour over the bream, cut the lemon peel into narrow strips, scatter over the top, cover and bake in a moderate oven (350°F, 180°C, gas mark 4) for 40 minutes or so.

For a change you can omit the tomatoes and use grated cheese instead. *Serves 4.*

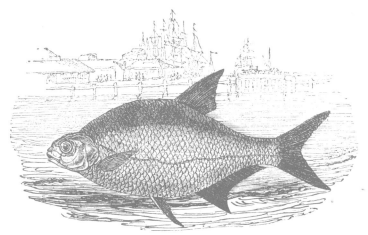

Char

74 Sometimes spelt 'charr', this fish was once most prolific in the Lake District and is, indeed, often referred to as 'Windermere char' although it is found in other deep waters in the Lake District as well as in Scotland and Ireland.

The char is a firm, white fleshed fish with a good flavour. It responds well to the simpler method of cooking – such as baking them in the oven on a bed of chopped onion, with a scattering of parsley, a seasoning of salt and pepper and a little butter.

Potted Char

Potted char was once as famous as Gentleman's Relish, and was made very simply by cleaning the fish, leaving on the heads, and baking in the oven 'till the eyes go white'. Then the fish was flaked off the bones, mixed with well-seasoned white sauce, pressed down in an earthenware jar and sealed with melted butter or mutton fat.

Fried Char

My only personal 'contact' with char was a memorable occasion when Fred Buller, dedicated angler, author of a tremendous tome on pike and co-author with Hugh Falkus of other fascinating books on fish and fishing, brought some Windermere char to my home, where Fred J. Taylor, volunteer chef, cooked it to a turn.

As far as I can remember on that 'night of nights' Fred seasoned some flour with salt and pepper, a pinch of cayenne and of allspice, rolled the cleaned and dried fish in this and simply fried them in butter.

Chub

Chub is a variety of carp. Due to the family habit of hibernating on the river bed in winter they do sometimes have a rather muddy flavour. This can easily be treated by soaking the fish in slightly salted water with a spoonful of vinegar. Then proceed with the cooking according to your recipe.

As the flesh of chub is, like the bream, rather coarse, insipid and bony, it needs a lot of flavouring. They can be cooked like carp but are mostly used in stews.

Stewed Chub

After cleaning and soaking in vinegar and water, take the flesh off the bones in fillets. Fry some onions in butter, add stock, a dessertspoon of mixed herbs and a tablespoon of Worcestershire sauce. Put in the fish, making sure you have added sufficient stock to cover them, and simmer for half an hour. Thicken the stew with white sauce (page 172) and serve with snippets of toast.

Alternatively, if the fish are small, the fillets can be dipped in egg and breadcrumbs and fried in hot fat.

In his book, *Troubled Waters*, my blithe and debonair friend, Maurice Wiggin, writes on cooking chub, 'if you are very pushed put it with any other fish handy (except bream) in a freshwater bouillabaisse'. But Maurice goes on: 'put on the table generous quantities of white wine. Failing that, beer or stout – and let joy be unrestrained'. He confesses that he's not sure he'd face 'the labour complexity and the smells' without something to drink (presumably strong enough to drown sensibilities). Now why did Maurice exclude bream? There is an old proverb: 'He that hath bream in his pond is able to bid his friends welcome.'

Those who have read Maurice Wiggin's delightful books will know that he is a wonderful wordsmith. True, he may not aspire to 'dripping gems divine into the golden chalice of a sonnet', but he does occasionally diversify and versify. I wrote to ask him for his recipe for freshwater bouillabaisse. Overleaf is his reply, *in toto*:

Freshwater Bouillabaisse

A freshwater bouillabaisse
Includes dace.
Even if you can't spell it
You can smell it.

There's a poet who deserves to lose his licence. I wrote it in a moment of careless rapture, but, in truth, dace would play no part in any dish of mine, though I *have* eaten them, many a time. But the flesh is a little too flaccid and bland, if you have anything better to serve.

Not everyone, of course, enjoys even the celebrated Mediterranean bouillabaisse of sea fish, which to be really genuine must include that curious and specialized fish called *rascasse*. Nor would I claim that all and sundry will enjoy the freshwater variation, but those who do enjoy it, enjoy it. The basic fishy ingredients, in my view, cohere around those two most tasty and nourishing of all the so-called 'coarse' fish – eels and gudgeon. I personally wouldn't bother, if eels and gudgeon weren't available. But a good variety of other fish make a perfectly acceptable contribution – perch, certainly, minnows if you can stoop so low, pike with the bones carefully removed, rudd, ruffe, and even, at a pinch, roach; though, like dace, roach lack character. But a good mixed bag of flavours is pretty well essential, and a lot of people would say that carp flesh is a *sine qua non*.

Clean and divide all the fish, whatever they are. Some in biggish firm chunks, some smaller and softer. With, say, approximately a couple of pounds of fish, you will need two large onions or their equivalent in little 'uns, sliced but not sliced small, a clove of garlic, four fair-sized tomatoes, skinned and pulped,

a bay leaf, a pinch of saffron if you like and can afford it, a little parsley and fennel, and enough oil to cover the pieces of fish as they lie in the pan, where you put them first. Classically it is olive oil, but you may prefer a less characterful substitute.

To make the bouillabaisse, first separate the larger, firmer pieces of fish from the softer, smaller pieces, which you 'reserve', as all cooks say. Pour the oil over the larger lumps, just covering them. Add the vegetables – to which you may add anything you fancy, such as sliced pepper, celery or cucumber, if you wish. (It's not cut-and-dried – the beauty of this dish is its experimental nature.)

Then pour boiling water over the whole lot and cook fairly furiously for 5 minutes. You must cook this first lot very fast. Then you add the softer, smaller fish pieces, and a generous glass of white wine, and boil the lot quite briskly for 7 minutes more.

To serve, pour off the liquid into soup plates or bowls with croûtons of fried bread. Put some of the fish flesh into the centre of each dish and sprinkle with parsley, adding diced cucumber if you like.

Put on the table as much first-rate white wine as you can afford. Or failing that, stout.

I first came across this notion in a fascinating book by Miss Margaret Butterworth, called *Now Cook me the Fish*, published many years ago by *Country Life*. I'm not sure how badly I have modified or mauled her original recipe – my copy was lent, lost or stolen years and years ago, and I have gone on messing about and modifying in my own meandering way. But, basically, it is a very interesting dish for people who really do like fish.

Fish Bubble and Squeak

My wife Kay the other day invented, or reinvented, a very simple, delicious fish dish – simply Fish Bubble-and-Squeak. Has anyone thought of this before? They must have – but we'd never heard of it.

It's simply the usual mixed-up leftovers of creamed potatoes and shredded cooked cabbage, with fish flesh flaked in – any fish you like, very nearly, provided it will flake up small. You break everything down small, mix well, use just a drop of milk and a dab of margarine to help bind the mixture – but only a drop – and fry hard in a hot heavy pan, in a very little fat, turning and mixing constantly with a wooden spatula, so that the dreamy brown fried bits are very numerous. Heavenly!

(Maurice Wiggin)

Water Souchy

I might mention here that in *The Wife's Own Book of Cookery* published about 1858 and compiled by Frederick Bishop there is a recipe for Water Souchy which, the writer says, 'is frequently seen upon the tables of the Blackwall and Greenwich hotels. It is composed of many kinds of fish (take perch, tench, carp or any small fish) cleaned, skinned and cut into pieces of equal size'. You should allow about 5 lb (2¼ kg) for 6 people.

The writer goes on: 'Make of parsley a faggot, slice parsley roots into slips, put them with salt and some whole peppers into sufficient water to cover the fish – simmer till the herbs are tender, put in the fish, stew gently ten minutes, removing any scum as it appears. Take out the fish, strain the liquor. Have ready some finely chopped parsley, put it in the liquor, give it a boil. Pour over the fish.' Then the writer says, rather naively, 'Brown and white bread should be sent to the table, to suit the taste of the partakers; epicures prefer the former.'

Dace

Dace appear to prefer English and Welsh waters – none of my Irish or Scottish friends seem to know them. They are edible, but some anglers consider them hardly worth the trouble of cooking, although when well cleaned, rolled in seasoned flour and fried in butter, then served with a squeeze of lemon and brown bread and butter, they make a tasty snack.

Spiced Dace

Slash each side of the dace. Mix together 1 teaspoon each of turmeric powder, chilli powder and garlic salt, add a pinch of cayenne, salt and black pepper and enough lemon juice to make a soft paste. Paint this over and inside the fish and well into the slits, roll in foil and bake in a moderate oven (350°F, 180°C, gas mark 4) for 20 minutes.

Potted Dace

dace
butter
nutmeg
freshly ground black pepper
Worcestershire sauce

Weigh any cooked, left over dace and flake it into small pieces. Melt an equal quantity of butter. Mix in the fish and season to taste with nutmeg, Worcestershire sauce and freshly ground black pepper. Put into small pots and chill until firm. Finally, pour a layer of clarified butter over each pot. Cover and store in the refrigerator. Serve with brown bread and butter and wedges of lemon.

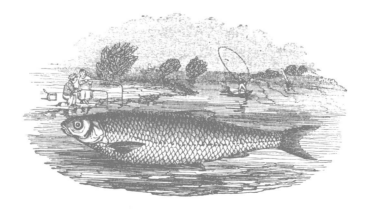

Flounder

This flat fish is found in abundance in English waters, mainly at the mouths of rivers. It is nutritious and easily digested. It should be cleaned and rubbed over with salt an hour or so before it is to be cooked. It can be boiled in stock to which salt and a little vinegar are added, or, even better, fried as described below.

Filet Duglere

A nineteenth-century French chef dreamed up this dish in which fillets of fish – which some chefs think might originally have been flounders – were cooked. Whatever the truth of the matter, they are certainly good served in this way.

6 fillets flounder
1 tablespoon minced shallot
2 tablespoons chopped parsley
3 tomatoes, skinned and seeds removed
salt and pepper
1pt (600ml) white wine
1 tablespoon flour
1 tablespoon butter

Into a buttered baking dish put the minced shallots, a tablespoon of chopped parsley and the prepared tomatoes. Dust the fish fillets with salt and pepper and lay them side by side on the mixture. Pour the white wine over them and bake in a fairly hot oven (375°F, 190°C, gas mark 5) for 20 minutes. Carefully remove the fillets to a serving dish and keep warm while finishing the sauce. Mix the flour to a paste with the butter. Add to the liquor and thicken over a low heat. Pour over the fillets and serve with a little more chopped parsley sprinkled over as a garnish. *Serves 4–6.*

Baked Flounder

Clean the fish, remove the bones and cut into fillets. Arrange these, skin side down, in a heat-proof dish. Sprinkle with dry mustard and arrange pieces of anchovy fillets over them. Melt 2oz (50g) butter, mix with the juice of a lemon, pour this over the fish and cook for 20–25 minutes in a moderate oven (350°F, 180°C, gas mark 4).

Flounder à la Meunière

4 whole flounder
seasoned flour or oatmeal
olive oil or butter

Roll the flounder in the seasoned flour. Fry until golden brown turning once. Serve right away with fresh parsley sprigs and lemon wedges, and, if you wish, Montpelier butter (page 177).

Grayling

And here and there a lusty trout
and here and there a grayling

William Brown wrote in 1616 that 'The Grayllynge, by another name called Ombre, is a delycyous fysshe to mannys mouthe'.

And in *The Compleat Angler*, Charles Cotton remarks that grayling, caught in the winter, is 'little inferior to the best trout'. It certainly has nice firm flesh with a delicate flavour.

The mention of grayling always conjures up for me the picture of Michael Barratt, on television, sitting down to what appeared a dainty dish of grayling, caught for him by Dick Walker and cooked for him by the chef of a well-known hotel in Fordingbridge. Perhaps the maternal instinct made me feel that he might have invited Dick to share the spoils.

First, of course, the fish must be cleaned, beheaded and the fins and scales removed.

Baked Grayling

This is perhaps the simplest way of cooking your grayling:

6 grayling
1½oz (40g) butter
a little flour
salt and pepper
¼pt (150ml) port wine
¼pt (150ml) water

Melt an ounce of the butter and mix it with flour and a little salt and pepper into a smooth paste and 'paint' this over the fish. Lay them in a well-buttered fireproof dish. Mix the port wine with the water, pour over the fish, cover with foil and bake in a moderate oven (350°F, 180°C, gas mark 4) for about 20 minutes. (If port wine is not available, use ½ pint/300ml red wine and no water.) *Serves 6.*

Stuffed Grayling

4 grayling
1 large onion, chopped
a few mushrooms
a little butter
2oz (50g) fresh breadcrumbs
grated rind and juice of 1 lemon
salt and pepper
pinch of thyme

For the stuffing, fry the chopped onion and mushrooms in a little butter. When soft, mix in the fresh breadcrumbs, and add the lemon juice and grated rind, salt, pepper and thyme. Stuff the fish, put in an ovenproof dish, spreading any surplus stuffing over. Cover and cook in a moderate oven (350°F, 180°C, gas mark 4) for about 25 minutes. *Serves 4.*

Grayling Gaillard

If you have large fish and want a 'special occasion' dish, clean and then fillet them. Dip the fillets in seasoned flour and fry in butter till browned on both sides. Then prepare the following sauce:

For the sauce

grated rind and juice of 1 orange
the juice of 1 lemon
2 egg yolks
¼pt (150ml) dry white wine or cider
4 tablespoons cream
salt
cayenne pepper
2oz (50g) butter

First grate the orange rind but put the juice only in the top of a double saucepan. Add the lemon juice and beat in gradually the egg yolks, dry white wine (or cider) and cream. When quite smooth, season with salt, a little cayenne pepper, add the grated orange rind and finally, off the heat and piece by piece, the butter. Pour over the fish in a suitable serving dish. *Serves 4.*

See photograph facing page 65

Grayling Aux Noisettes

6 grayling, about 8oz (225g) each
flour
pinch of salt
oil
lemon juice
3 tablespoons butter
4oz (100g) flaked almonds
2oz (50g) chopped hazelnuts
Maître d'Hotel butter (page 177)

Clean and gut the grayling and sprinkle them lightly with seasoned flour. Heat the oil in a heavy frying pan, and when it is very hot cook the grayling for 5 minutes on each side. Sprinkle them with lemon juice and transfer them to a serving dish. Keep warm.

Melt the butter in a small pan. Add the almonds and hazelnuts and stir them over a good heat until they turn golden. Do not allow them to burn.

Pour the butter and nuts over the grayling in the serving dish, season with salt and pepper, and serve with Maître d'Hotel butter. *Serves 6.*

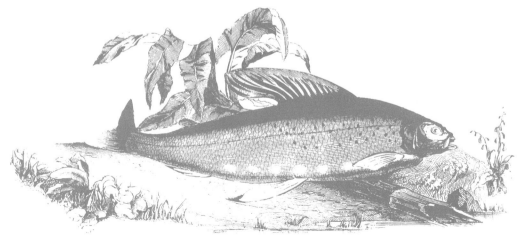

Gudgeon

Gudgeon, a small but well-flavoured fish, is at its best from midsummer to late autumn.

Arthur Smith, author of *The Thames Angler*, wrote, 'I know of no greater delicacy for supper than a dish of gudgeon nicely fried. They are easy of digestion and considered a very wholesome food.'

But John Gay evidently took a dim view of gudgeon. He wrote:

What gudgeon are we men
Every woman's easy prey!
Though we've felt the hook, – again
We bite – and they betray.

Deep Fried Gudgeon

The best way to cook them, after cleaning thoroughly, is to dry them, dip in milk, coat them well with flour, put them into a wire frying basket (first shaking off surplus flour) and cook them till crisp like potato chips. You can pretty them up with a light dusting of paprika or pep them up with a suspicion of cayenne. Sprinkle over some lemon juice, put strips of lemon rind around the dish and serve with brown bread and butter.

Jack Hargreaves, who is known and admired by all of us, has written:
I think the tastiest thing I ever ate that came out of fresh water is the gudgeon. Long ago I used to go and fish the Bedfordshire Ooze with Bobby St John Cooper. I used to get up first thing in the morning and go and stand in the small river in gum boots and kick up the silt. When you did this the gudgeon all lined up in a v-shaped shoal about twenty yards below you and you could trot a maggot down to them and catch almost as many as you liked. I used to slip out first thing and come back with a bucketful. By the time I arrived back Bobby had the camp fire going and a frying pan. We cooked them completely fresh. You chop off their heads with a penknife, run your thumb down them to clean them and then drop them in the fat. The result is absolutely delicious. I don't know if this is what they used to call Gudgeon Tansy – I know there was such a dish – but I can tell you that it was a delicacy.

Mullet

Mullet is seldom seen in modern fish shops, but if an angler is successful in landing some they are well worth taking a little trouble over and will make quite a succulent dish if cooked while fresh.

Small ones are excellent grilled whole. First scale and clean them, then score the flesh deeply a few times on either side. Brush them with olive oil or melted butter, grill them and serve them with Hollandaise (page 177) or Piquant (page 172) sauce.

Baked Mullet

2 mullet, about 1lb (450g) each
olive oil
dry white wine
a sprig of fennel or a bay leaf
salt and pepper
12 stoned black olives
slices of lemon

In this French method, clean the fish, put them into an ovenproof dish and pour over just sufficient olive oil and dry white wine to cover – in the proportion of 2 parts oil to 1 part wine. Add the fennel or bay leaf, salt and pepper and bake, uncovered, in a moderate oven (350°F, 180°C, gas mark 4) for about 20 minutes, basting occasionally if necessary. Remove from the oven, then dot over with the stoned black olives, return to the oven and cook 5 more minutes. Serve with lemon slices. *Serves 4.*

Perch

The name perch is said to derive from *pesce persico*, its origin being in ancient Persia, but other references maintain that it was first discovered in Greece.

The flesh is firm and white, nutritious and easily digested. A writer named Gesner stated that German physicians considered perch so wholesome that fever patients were allowed to eat it when no other food could be taken.

It is best caught from running streams, but if taken from lakes or ponds, it may taste slightly muddy.

Start by removing the fins, and be very careful as they are needle-sharp, cut off the head and tail, take out the entrails, then plunge into boiling water for a few minutes, after which it is easy to remove the scales. Rub some salt into the cavity and put the fish into cold salted water, if caught in still water.

Francis Francis, author of *Angling Reminiscences*, claims that his way of cooking perch is the best way of all. He writes:

Now shall you see some real sportsman's cookery. Give me half a dozen perch and a copy of *The Times* newspaper. Take each perch, wiping him dry, without cutting or scraping him in the least, as that would break the skin and let out the juices; then take a piece of paper, wet it in the lake, roll the perch in three or four folds, screw up the ends and thrust perch, paper and all into the embers. In from five to ten minutes, your fish will be cooked. Rake him out, take off the charred paper, remove his scales, which will come off *en masse*; rub the white succulent sides with butter, pepper and salt to taste; make an incision along the backbone and flake off the beautiful firm white flesh; turn the carcase over and serve the other side in the same way; throw away the bones and interior and eat the remainder. It is a dish for a King or an angler.

Stuffed Baked Perch

If the fish are large, say 2½–3lb (1¼–1½kg), I suggest you bake them as follows:

4oz (100g) breadcrumbs
1oz (25g) suet
grated rind and juice of 1 lemon
1 teaspoon mixed herbs
2 teaspoons freshly chopped parsley
salt and pepper
a little milk
1oz (25g) butter

Mix together 3oz (75g) of the breadcrumbs, suet, the grated lemon rind, mixed herbs and freshly chopped parsley, and season with salt and pepper. Bind with a little milk. Put this into the fish, place them in a greased baking dish and sprinkle over the remaining breadcrumbs, pour over the lemon juice and ¼ pint (150ml) water, dot with butter, cover and bake in a moderate oven (350°F, 180°C, gas mark 4) for 20 minutes. *Serves 4–6.*

Some time ago, a former Duke of Bedford (who had a private zoo at Woburn) imported from Austria some fish which were called pike-perch. They were renamed the zander and I believe there are now large numbers in the East Anglian Water Authority's area. If any came my way, I would try baking them like perch.

Roach & Tench

The roach, we are told, 'is of little estimation for the table', but in any case it should not be eaten before the beginning of August or after the end of March. Careful cooking can make it palatable. It should be cleaned and scaled, care being taken to avoid being pierced by the needle-sharp bones.

The author of *The Thames Angler* maintains that the tench is called the fish's physician because of the healing properties it is said to possess. It must be cleaned, scaled and soaked in salt water.

It is generally considered best stewed, fried or baked (stuffed) like carp, but it is equally good cooked like roach. Small specimens can be fried in hot fat.

Baked Roach

3lb (1½kg) whole fish
butter
shallots or onion
parsley
salt and pepper
¼pt (150ml) dry white wine
¼pt (150ml) double cream

Butter generously an ovenproof dish and cover the base with chopped onions or shallots. Scatter over them parsley, salt and pepper, lay in the fish and dot with butter. Cover and bake in a fairly hot oven (400°F, 200°C, gas mark 6) for 15 minutes. Add the white wine, put back in the oven for a few minutes, then pour over sufficient cream to cover and cook for another 5 minutes before serving. *Serves 6.*

Tench is also good cooked in this way.

Boiled Roach

Put in a stewpan 1 quart (1 litre) of water with ¼ pint (150ml) vinegar, salt, pepper, a *bouquet garni* and a tablespoon of grated horseradish. Bring to the boil, put in the fish, turn down heat and simmer 15–20 minutes. Serve with a sauce (either onion or caper would be good – see Chapter 14).

Stewed Tench

For great occasions stew the tench in a little good stock with a glass of claret for 30 minutes. Drain and put on a hot dish and cover with halved cooked oysters. Thicken some of the liquor with a *beurre manié* of flour and butter, season with salt and pepper and pour over.

Failing oysters, open a tin of lobster or crab meat and use this instead.

Some Mixed Fish Recipes

If there are any doubts as to whether the smaller freshwater fish are worth the time and trouble involved in cooking and serving as the main dish of a meal, they can certainly be utilized as economical components or accessories.

Left-over chunks of salmon and trout are often made into kedgeree, soufflés, etc, and there is no reason why the flesh of lesser fry should not be used in much the same way. (See, for example, the recipes for Salmon Kedgeree, page 21, and Salmon Soufflé, page 22.)

The first thing in such schemes is to get the flesh free of bones and having cleaned the fish in the usual way and soaked it in salt water for some hours, put it into a pan of cold water with a cup of vinegar, bring to the boil, turn the heat down and let it simmer until the fish appears to be breaking up, usually after about 1–1½ hours. Let it cool, lift out the fish and it should then be easy to remove the flesh from the bones. Realizing that, apart from its nutritional value, it has little actual flavour, it will need 'pepping up' with accompaniments of herbs, spices and sauces.

Fish Mould

1lb (450g) cooked, flaked fish
½pt (300ml) *béchamel* sauce (page 172)
2 eggs, well beaten
¼pt (150ml) cream
2 tablespoons chives, minced
2 tablespoons parsley, minced
salt and pepper

Mix the flaked fish with the *béchamel* sauce, add the beaten eggs, cream, chives, parsley, salt and pepper. Put into a buttered mould, stand in a baking tin of hot water and cook in a hot oven (400°F, 200°C, gas mark 6) for 30 minutes. Chill, turn out and serve with a piquant sauce (page 172). *Serves 4.*

Scalloped Fish

½lb (225g) cooked, flaked fish
1 green pepper, finely sliced
a little butter
2 tablespoons flour
⅓pt (200ml) double cream
4 tablespoons white breadcrumbs
salt and pepper
1 wine glass sherry

Fry the green pepper in butter until soft. Stir in the flour, then add the cream gradually. Stir till smooth and thick then add the flaked fish, 2 tablespoons of breadcrumbs, salt and pepper and sherry. Put in a baking dish, sprinkle over the remaining 2 tablespoons breadcrumbs, dot with butter and bake for 30 minutes in a moderate oven (350°F, 180°C, gas mark 4). *Serves 3–4 as a first course.*

Fish à la Portugaise

1lb (450g) cooked, flaked fish

For the mushroom sauce

½lb (225g) mushrooms, sliced
1oz (25g) butter
1 tablespoon tomato purée
1 tablespoon flour
½pt (300ml) stock
chopped parsley
1 dessertspoon brown sugar
1 tablespoon dry white wine

First cook and flake the fish. Make the sauce by frying the sliced mushrooms in butter, add the tablespoon each of tomato purée and flour, stir in ½ pint of stock (or crumble a stock cube in ½ pint/300ml hot water) with a little chopped parsley and a dessertspoon of brown sugar. Stir well, bring to the boil, add a tablespoon of dry white wine and pour over the fish. Cover and bake in a moderate oven (350°F, 180°C, gas mark 4) for 25–30 minutes. Serve with potatoes. *Serves 3–4.*

Fish with Curry

1lb (450g) cooked flaked fish
½pt (300ml) *béchamel* sauce (page 172)
1 teaspoon Worcestershire sauce
few drops Tabasco sauce
the juice of 1 lemon
1 dessertspoon curry powder
salt and pepper
pinch of cayenne pepper
butter
1oz (25g) breadcrumbs

Make ½ pint (300ml) *béchamel* sauce, add to it the Worcestershire sauce, a few drops only of Tabasco sauce, the lemon juice, the curry powder mixed to a paste with a little water, salt and a pinch of cayenne pepper. Butter a casserole dish, put half the sauce in the bottom, then cover with the flaked fish and finally the rest of the sauce. Sprinkle with the breadcrumbs, previously fried in butter until crisp, and bake in a moderate oven (350°F, 180°C, gas mark 4) for 25–30 minutes or till nicely browned. Serve with boiled rice. *Serves 6.*

Fish Soufflé

½lb (225g) cooked, flaked fish
2oz (50g) white breadcrumbs
grated rind and juice of 1 lemon
1 tablespoon minced thyme
salt and pepper
¼pt (150ml) milk
1 egg, separated

Flake the cooked fish, mix with the bread-crumbs, the grated rind of the lemon and minced thyme. Season with salt and pepper. Add the milk and cook over low heat for 10 minutes, stirring from time to time. Separate the egg, beat the yolk, and add this to the mixture with the juice of the lemon. Finally, fold in the whipped egg white, put the mixture in a buttered soufflé dish and bake in a hot oven (425°F, 210°C, gas mark 7) for 15 minutes.

For a change, you could cook the soufflé in a ring mould, then turn it out very carefully and fill the centre with seasoned whipped cream to which you have added any available seafood (lobster, crab, prawns or shrimps). *Serves 4 as a first course.*

Fish Mousse

½lb (225g) cooked, flaked fish
6 fl. oz (200ml) dry white wine
4oz (100g) white breadcrumbs
2oz (50g) butter, melted
salt and pepper
2 eggs, separated

Mix the flaked fish with the white wine, breadcrumbs and melted butter, salt and pepper. Beat the 2 egg yolks and add to the fish mixture, then whip the egg whites until stiff and fold in. Put in a buttered soufflé dish, stand in a baking dish of hot water and cook for 25–30 minutes in a fairly hot oven (400°F, 200°C, gas mark 6). *Serves 4.*

Savoury Fish Supper

¾–1lb (350–450g) cooked, flaked fish
3 rashers lean bacon, chopped
1lb (450g) cooked potato
5 tablespoons cream
2oz (50g) butter
½lb (225g) cooked green peas
grated rind of 1 lemon
pinch of thyme
salt and pepper

This is best served with pieces of fish previously dipped in batter and deep-fried.

Fry the chopped bacon until crisp. Mash the potatoes with the cream and butter, add the cooked green peas, fried bacon, grated lemon rind and season with a pinch of thyme, salt and pepper. Finally stir in the flaked fish. *Serves 6.*

Fish Pie

Almost every cookery book which includes recipes for fish produces one for fish pie – from the classic and the simple to the most elaborate. This is one of the simplest.

½lb (225g) cooked, flaked fish
½lb (225g) mashed potato
1oz (25g) softened butter
1 egg, beaten
salt and pepper
butter
2oz (50g) fried breadcrumbs

Combine the flaked fish with the mashed potatoes, softened butter and beaten egg, and season well with salt and pepper. Put in a buttered pie dish, cover with the browned breadcrumbs, dot with butter and bake in a fairly hot oven (375°F, 190°C, gas mark 5) for 20 minutes or until golden brown.

VARIATIONS

1 Use 4oz (100g) mashed potatoes and 4oz (100g) suet with ½lb (225g) of fish, well-seasoned and combined with 2 beaten eggs. Continue to cook as for the basic recipe given above.

2 If you wish to go a bit further, you can add ¼ pint (150ml) sherry to the mixture and lay one or two bay leaves on top. Cook as above.

3 Finally, here is a more ambitious variation on the basic theme.

12oz (350g) flaked fish
½pt (300ml) *béchamel* sauce (page 172)
salt and pepper
2oz (50g) grated cheese
2oz (50g) peeled shrimps
1 teaspoon dry mustard
2 hard-boiled eggs
2oz (50g) breadcrumbs
butter

First make ½ pint (300ml) *béchamel* sauce (page 172), season with salt and pepper, and add the grated cheese, peeled shrimps, dry mustard and hard-boiled eggs, chopped. Stir in the flaked fish, sprinkle over the breadcrumbs (or alternatively cover with a layer of mashed potatoes), dot with butter and bake in a moderate oven (350°F, 180°C, gas mark 4) for 25–30 minutes.

If you like mushrooms, you can substitute these, chopped and fried in butter for a few minutes, for the cheese.

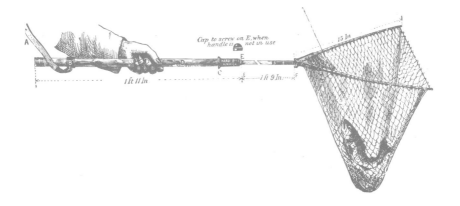

Ceviche

12oz (350g) cooked, flaked fish
2 tablespoons lemon juice
1 clove garlic, minced *or* 1 medium onion
2 tomatoes, skinned, de-seeded and chopped
1 small red pepper, chopped
salt
chilli powder
¼pt (150ml) dry white wine
a few green olives, pitted

To make this Mexican dish, flake the cooked fish and marinate it for a few hours or overnight in the lemon juice. Mix together the minced clove of garlic with the tomatoes and chopped red pepper. Add the wine and salt and chilli powder to taste. Stir in the fish and lemon juice marinade and garnish with a few green olives. *Serves 3–4 as a first course.*

If not just for family consumption, it might be advisable to substitute an onion for the garlic.

See also the recipes for Freshwater Bouillabaisse (page 76), Fish Bubble-and-Squeak (page 77), and Water Souchy (page 77).

As agreed, the flesh of coarse fish is often almost devoid of flavour, so besides a seasoning of salt and pepper, it is advisable to give it a boost, and this can be done by the addition of, say, chopped parsley, dill, or other herbs, or a little sauce like anchovy, soy or Worcestershire, tomato purée, minced onion, garlic or gherkins. (See sauces section for other ideas.) As potatoes are often a main ingredient, serve with other vegetables, like green peas, braised celery or spinach.

And to end this chapter, I quote from a gravestone in a Ripon churchyard:

Here lies poor, but honest Bryan Tunstall.
He was a most expert angler, until Death,
envious of his merit, threw out his line,
hooked him and landed him here.
The 21st day of April 1790.

6
Eels

Introduction

For centuries it was something of a mystery as to how eel propagation occurred, since they apparently contained neither roe nor milt. However, a Danish biologist finally tracked down their spawning grounds and it is now known that these are in or near the Sargasso Sea, from which the larvae travel, it is thought, back to the rivers whence their parents came.

In fresh water they grow to full maturity, when under some mysterious compulsion they return to the Sargasso to spawn and then to die.

There has, in the past, been some controversy as to whether eels are really a desirable food. *Regimen Sanitalis Salernia* states:

Who knows not physic should be nice in choice
In eating Eels, because they hurt the voice;
Both Eels and cheese, without good store of wine
Well drunk with them, offend at any time.

Today, however, there is no doubt that eel is a much-prized delicacy. They are at their best during autumn and winter. The flesh is rich, with a subtle flavour best enhanced by the judicious use of herbs and spices.

To skin an Eel

If you should be presented, by an angling husband or friend, with a live eel, it is to be hoped you are not squeamish, because men have a way of opting out of unpleasant duties.

To skin an eel, it is necessary to hold it firmly by its head, preferably at your shoulder height. Those who deal with considerable numbers of eels have a nail with its head cut off and the end sharpened, driven into the wall. The dead eel is pushed on to this, the nail passing in at one eye and out at the other. Alternatively, a small butcher's hook (S-hook) can be used, the eel being attached in the same way and the other end of the hook caught over something convenient.

A third way is to use a loop of stout string round the eel, just behind the pectoral fins. It must be pulled very tight.

Having suspended the eel in one of these ways, take a knife with a sharp edge but a blunt back. An ordinary penknife is satisfactory. Push the end of the blade into the skin just behind the pectoral fins, with the knife at right angles to the eel; that is, with the flat of the blade horizontal and the eel hanging straight down. Do not point the knife straight at the middle of the eel, but aim to run the blade round the eel with its point just under the skin, sharp edge outwards. If the knife is sharp, but its back blunt, you can cut all round without sticking the knife into the flesh.

Having cut all round, grip the edge of the skin with pliers or artery forceps and pull downwards a little way. Change the grip and pull again, going round the cut edge of the skin until it is rolled back by about half an inch all round – it will look rather like a roll-neck pullover.

Wrap a coarse cloth or piece of sacking round the rolled-back skin and, gripping firmly with the inner sides of thumb and forefinger, pull downwards. The skin will come off in one long pull.

There is very little meat at the tail-end, for about 3–5 inches (8–13 cm), depending on the size of the eel, so this, with the head, can be cut off and the guts removed.

The heads and tails, with the skins, can be stewed separately to produce a stock which will jellify when reduced, and can be used as a base for jellying the eels, but most cooks prefer to make a jelly with gelatine and fish stock.

Eels have been popular for a long time. *The Accomplish't Lady's Delight*, written just 300 years ago, tells us how to 'Souce' an eel:

To Souce an Eel

Souce an Eel with a handful of Salt, split it down the back, take out the Chine-bone, season the Eel with nutmeg, Pepper, Salt and sweet herbs minc'd; then lay a pack thread at each end, and the middle roul up like a Collar of Brawn; then boyl it in water, Salt and Vinegar, a blade or two of Mace, and half a slice of Lemon, boyl it half an hour, keep it in the same Liquor two or three days, then cut it out in round pieces, and lay six or seven in a Dish with Parsley and Barberries, and serve it with Vinegar in Saucers.

Eel Pie From Eel-Pie Island

Although I have never made, nor even seen, an eel pie, I lived, for a time, at Kingston-on-Thames, and a favourite rendezvous was at Eel-Pie Island in the river at Twickenham. This eyot was once famous for its eel pies made from a recipe in *The Cook's Oracle* by Dr William Kitchiner, published in 1843. It is as follows:

2 Thames eels, skinned and chopped into
   2-inch pieces
2 shallots or small onions
a little butter
1 dessertspoon chopped parsley
pinch of nutmeg
salt and pepper
2 wineglasses sherry
flour or cornflour
the juice of 1 lemon
2 hardboiled eggs, quartered
12oz (350g) puff pastry

Fry the shallots or small onions in a little butter, add the chopped parsley, nutmeg, salt and pepper and sherry. After 5 minutes cooking, put the eel in and add sufficient water to cover, bring to the boil and then simmer for half an hour.

Lift out the eel and thicken the stock with flour or cornflour mixed with a little water, add the lemon juice and cook for a few minutes more. Arrange the eel in a pie dish with the quartered hardboiled eggs, pour over the sauce and set aside till cold. Cover with puff pastry and bake first in a hot oven (400°F, 200°C, gas mark 6) for 20 minutes to raise this and then lower the heat to 350°F, 180°C, gas mark 4. Cook 1 hour in all. *Serves 6–8.*

For home consumption, a simpler pie can be made by first making a forcemeat with 4oz (100g) suet, 4oz (100g) breadcrumbs, 2oz (50g) chopped anchovies (or a tablespoonful of anchovy sauce), a pinch of mace and of nutmeg, salt and pepper. Beat an egg, mix with a little milk and bind the stuffing with this. Put a layer in the pie dish, then the eels, the rest of the forcemeat, scatter with chopped parsley, cover with pastry and bake for an hour. And if you don't want to make pastry, cover with mashed potatoes.

Cuisine d'Amour

In many lands, eels have been credited with aphrodisiacal qualities and the chef of a once famous house in Paris considered this recipe to have 'exciting virtues'.

Cut a skinned eel into short pieces, cover them generously with truffles, wrap in buttered paper and bake in a hot oven. Season well with cayenne and serve on a bed of crayfish tails, which have been stewed in white wine.

As the name implies, this was considered something of a love potion.

Perhaps, in some cases, it was wishful thinking but oysters and various crustaceans have also, at times, become popular for reasons other than appeasing the appetite. For one, Casanova wrote that he owned most of his amorous successes to the supper of hot spiced shrimps his mother consumed just before his birth, in Venice in 1725.

Escoffier, perhaps the most famous of all French chefs and *Maître* at the Carlton Hotel, London, at the turn of the century, wrote, 'In England eels are considered common and are principally used in the preparation of a pie held in high esteem by the frequenters of coffee-shops along the banks of the Thames'.

Well, times change, but in the days of my youth, on a trip to London's East End, the small café where we had lunched offered only two dishes, stewed eels (hot) or jellied eels (cold). We sat on forms at trestle tables and consumed the stewed eels, in a parsley sauce to which we added salt, pepper and vinegar, and it was delicious. Although smoked eels are now popular in London's West End hotels and restaurants at fabulous prices and fetching £6–£7 apiece on the waterfront in Amsterdam, I have read that tons of jellied eels are still sold from stalls and barrows on the East Side.

Reg Varney, that well-loved actor (of *On the Buses* and *Down the Gate*) has said, 'I grew up eating jellied eels. It was a regular meal, because it was such a cheap dish and we didn't have much money to spare.'

Charles Wade, former Director of The Anglers' Co-operative Association, complains that even when eels are dead they won't lie down. 'Cut them into chunky pieces,' he says, 'put them into a frying pan and they keep doing a weird vibrating conga to the rhythm of the sizzling fat.'

Pytchley Eels

This recipe for stewed eels was published just about 100 years ago and is richer than the one we enjoyed.

2 eels, 1lb (450g) each
flour
¼pt (150ml) hock or cider
½pt (300ml) red wine
1 whole onion
a little grated horseradish
half a dozen button mushrooms
1 dessertspoon anchovy sauce
1 bay leaf
salt and pepper
a squeeze of lemon juice
1 dessertspoon cornflour

Skin and wash the two eels, dry them thoroughly and cut into 2-inch (5cm) pieces, flour them and put in a stewpan with the hock or cider, red wine, onion, horseradish, mushrooms, anchovy sauce and bay leaf. Simmer for 30 minutes, then take out the fish and the onion. Add the salt, pepper, and a squeeze of lemon juice to the cooking liquor and then thicken it with the cornflour mixed with a little cold water. Put the eels back into the sauce and keep hot until ready to serve. *Serves 6.*

Matelote of Eels

This French stewed eel dish is much more elaborate than London's simple version.

2 eels, 1lb (450g) each
butter for frying
1pt (600ml) dry white wine
1 clove garlic, crushed
2 onions, chopped
1 carrot, chopped
pinch of mace
pinch of mixed herbs
1 egg
¼pt (150ml) cream

Skin and wash the eels and cut into 2-inch (5cm) pieces. Fry the eel pieces in butter for about 10 minutes, then add the white wine, crushed clove of garlic, chopped onions and carrot, mace and herbs. Cover and simmer for 25 minutes. Beat the egg and cream together and add sufficient of the cooking liquid from the eels – about ¼ pint (150ml) – to make a sauce. Cook over a low flame and do not allow to come near to boiling point. Lay pieces of eel on fried bread croûtons and pour the sauce over. *Serves 6.*

Sometimes button mushrooms or soaked prunes, or even seedless raisins, are cooked and used as a garnish, and cider can be substituted for the wine.

Escoffier did deign to include some recipes for eels in his instructions to assistant chefs. Opposite are two of them.

Catigau d'Anguilles

This delicious recipe is very popular in Provence.

2 eels, 1lb (450g) each
4 slices lean bacon, chopped
a little olive oil
½ lb (225g) onions, sliced
½ lb (225g) white of leek, sliced
½ lb (225g) tomatoes, peeled and chopped
2 cloves garlic, crushed
1 bay leaf
salt and pepper
1lb (450g) potatoes
stock
freshly ground black pepper

Fry the pieces of bacon in a little olive oil till cooked, then add the sliced onions and leeks. When these are sufficiently soft add the peeled and chopped tomatoes, garlic, bay leaf, salt and pepper. On top of this put a layer of sliced raw potatoes and the skinned eel cut in thick slices. Add sufficient stock to cover and boil rapidly for 20 minutes. Usually the stock is poured over pieces of French bread in a deep dish, and the eel and vegetables, liberally seasoned with freshly ground black pepper, are served separately. *Serves 6.*

If you don't want an elaborate dish, a simple meal can be made by just coating the eel pieces in egg and breadcrumbs and frying in hot fat or grilling and serving with *sauce tartare* (page 178).

Eels au Vert

2 eels, 1lb (450g) each
2oz (50g) parsley, finely chopped
2oz (50g) chervil, finely chopped
2oz (50g) tender nettle, finely chopped
a few leaves of sage and thyme
2oz (50g) butter
1pt (600ml) dry white wine
salt and pepper
4 egg yolks

Stew the finely chopped parsley, chervil, tender nettle, sage and thyme in the butter for 20 minutes. Meanwhile cut the skinned eel into pieces 2 inches long. Add to the herbs with the white wine, salt and pepper. Cook for 20 minutes longer, then thicken with the 4 egg yolks and set aside. This should be served very cold. *Serves 4.*

I've wondered where Escoffier, working in London, obtained his tender nettle. Fortunately, spinach is easily available, either fresh or frozen, and there is little difference in the flavour when cooked.

Izaak Walton's Eels

'First, wash him in water and salt; then pull off his skin below his vent or navel and not much further; having done that, take out his guts as clean as you can, but wash him not; then give him three or four scotches with a knife and then put into his belly and those scotches, sweet herbs, an anchovy and a little nutmeg grated or cut very small and your herbs and anchovies must also be cut very small and mixt with good butter and salt; having done this, then pull his skin over him, all but his head, which you are to cut off, to the end you may tie his skin about that part where his head grew and it must be so tied as to keep all his moisture within his skin: and having done this tie him with tape or pachthread to a spit and roast him leisurely and baste him with water and salt till his skin breaks and then with butter; and having roasted him enough, let what was put in his belly and what he drips, be his sauce.'

See also the recipe for smoked eel (page 36).

Fried Elvers

Since Roman times, the very young eels, called elvers, have been considered a delicacy and, in the West of England, dishes made from elvers, which are abundant in the river Severn, are extremely popular. They are usually cooked like whitebait. That is, they are washed several times in salt water to remove any slime, then coated with seasoned flour, put in a wire chip basket (after being shaken well to remove surplus flour) and fried in boiling fat, just like potato crisps, and served with lemon and brown bread and butter.

Elver Omelette

Fry 1lb (450g) of elvers in dripping or seasoned lard till they turn white, then pour over them 2 well-beaten eggs and cook them, like an omelette, lifting edges around the pan till set.

Like the full-grown eels, elvers can also be baked in a pie and, incidentally, they are considered by some anglers as the best bait for chub and, in swift water, for perch. But the latest report on elvers is that the Japanese have decided they are a reliable aphrodisiac and in the last elver season (which lasts only 2 months) 100 tons were flown to Japan. They have also become popular on the Continent. No doubt in the future we shall be having eel farms in England.

Part Two

Game

Introduction

Who doth ambition shun
And loves to live i' th' sun
Seeking the food he eats
And pleased with what he gets.

Shakespeare

Sport has been classified as something which is a diversion from work, but sport which involves killing fish, birds and animals is instinctive in man, stemming from the millions of years during which his life depended on what he could kill by hunting or fishing. Now that civilization has made this no longer a necessity, the urge to pit one's wits against nature and to excel is still with us.

Before the Saxons came to Britain, hunting and fishing was considered the common right of every man, but from then onwards, barbaric penalties were imposed on poachers in royal hunting grounds or enclosed parks – from the loss of a right hand to death even.

Various monarchs have encouraged sport. Canute made archery compulsory. William the Conqueror went for the tourney and joust. As far back as 1410, Edward (Second Duke of York) was called 'The Master of Game'. He went coursing with dogs and wrote about 'the hounds that hunt by scent. I will begin with raches and their nature and then greyhounds and their nature'. Henry VIII liked hawking and fencing and it was under him that horse-racing first made its appearance. James I also became a devotee of horse-racing and the first official race-course was opened at Chester. Although Cromwell put a temporary stop to sport of all kinds, Charles II encouraged it, especially horse-racing. He had his own course at Windsor, but he loved Newmarket, where his favourite stallion, Rowley, had set up a sensational record of prowess,

both on and off the course. A part of Newmarket race-course is still called the Rowley Mile and I believe the Rowley Stakes are still held there. It is said that when Charles learned that he had been nicknamed Old Rowley by the populace, he regarded it as a great compliment. He was also called the 'Father of the Turf', while Isaak Walton, who published *The Compleat Angler* about the same time, was dubbed the 'Father of Angling'. Charles was himself an enthusiastic angler.

We are not taught in school that Queen Anne was a great sportswoman (from history lessons I can only recall that she had nineteen children and outlived them all). But it was she who laid out the Royal Ascot Race-course and, despite the fact that she was obese and suffered from gout, she would travel to the races at York, which was her favourite course. She also influenced the importation of Arab horses.

Perhaps the most fantastic of English sportswomen was Dame Juliana Berners, Prioress of Sopewell Abbey, who in 1450 produced a book on sport entitled *The Boke of St Albans* (sometimes called *The Treatysse*) which showed vast experience of hawking, hunting and fly-fishing. Incidentally, it was at Dame Juliana's nunnery that Henry VIII married Anne Boleyn.

It may interest sportsmen not already familiar with poor blind Milton's *Paradise Regained* that he visualized Satan's temptation in the wilderness as:

A table richly spread in regal mode,
With dishes piled and meats of noblest sort
And savour; beasts of chase, or fowl or game
In pastry built, or from the spit or boiled.
Gris-amber steamed; all fish
From sea or shore, freshet or purling brook.

A short time ago, a lively discussion took place at my home, as to what is game and what is sport. Friends from South Africa seemed to think mostly in terms of elephants, rhinoceros and hippopotami. Indeed one volunteered this recipe for my book:

Take one medium-sized elephant, cut into small pieces, cook in rich gravy for four weeks at 465 degrees. This should serve 3800 meals, but if not sufficient, add two rabbits.

Big game is now protected in safari parks, but some African tribes, especially the Kavangos, who live close to waters where hippos abound, are allowed to kill one each year for a special feast. The tribal chief shoots this at close range with a heavy rifle and since the poor animal is a sitting (or rather, slow-swimming) target, it cannot be regarded as sport. However, mention of it should perhaps be made since hippo meat is considered a great delicacy. The local chief first chops off the tail, which is cooked specially for his favourite wife. His senior adviser then cuts himself a slice, after which it is a chop-chop free-for-all. The meat, skin and bone is all cooked over open fires in vast cauldrons, accompanied by huge vessels filled with beer. Tribesmen from far and wide join in the feast, and a good time is had by all. But we are not concerned with the big game of the Dark Continent, so let our conversation come back to the game and sport of Great Britain.

Someone said game meant esculent birds that live in freedom and another added that deer, hare and rabbits are also fair game. We agreed that catching or shooting any of these creatures was justified if the result was edible food and that, if left to breed unchecked, they would be detrimental to the human population.

It was decided unanimously that to hunt or destroy any dumb creature just 'for the fun of it' was not sportsmanship.

But for some reason, during this meeting, and due to the peculiar working of the brain, an old song kept going through my mind. It has nothing to do with cooking, but it may amuse my readers:

I was twelve years old when some friends from London escorted me around to see the

sights of London, the Crown Jewels and the Bloody Tower, Madame Tussaud's and the Chamber of Horrors, and as many other places and things as possible which they thought would interest a growing schoolgirl. And that included my very first music hall, the Metropolitan in Edgware Road (where Marie Lloyd became famous). I can only recall two of the turns that night and they are indelibly etched on my memory. One was announced as Henri De Vries Living Statues. The curtain went up and there on the stage against a black velvet background was a group of people, standing on a sort of plinth and supporting a large bowl. I think it was a reproduction of a famous fountain, but I never knew, because they were all stark naked (though covered in whitewash or something), but to the naive little girl from 'down on the farm' it was a shocker. I closed my eyes tightly and stayed in a state of suspended animation until I heard laughter and a voice shouting, 'Bang, bang, bang', which restored my circulation, and I opened my eyes to see an oddly dressed female with a gun. She sang:

At five o'clock this morning, the dawn was breaking red
When I put on my shooting boots and shot – right out of bed.
With pockets full of cartridges I strolled across the lea,
While I was after partridges, the Squire was after me.
And, heavens, what we shot! I'll tell you what we got.

Sixteen beaters, a keeper and a cow;
A postman, a dustman, the barmaid at the Plough.
What shots! Pot shots! And how the welkin rang;
Oh! What a wonderful day we had. Bang, bang, bang!!

I'm afraid I've forgotten the rest but that was my first sight of Nellie Wallace, who went on to become a famous and much loved comedienne.

Let's get back to the cook-stove.

Hanging Game

Generally speaking, all game should be hung where there is a current of fresh air for a few days before plucking and drawing. This not only makes them more tender but improves the flavour. The time allowed for hanging depends, of course, on the climatic conditions prevailing, but in warm, 'muggy' weather, not more than three or four days. In cold,

damp weather, about five to seven days is sufficient, although any bird badly bruised, or bleeding, should be cooked as soon as possible.

Snipe, woodcock, golden and grey plovers (the only kind of plovers not protected) should be cooked without hanging and French chefs maintain they should not be drawn, due to differences in their internal arrangements.

Plucking

This operation should be carried out somewhere where flying feathers will be immaterial. You will probably find it easiest to put on a large apron and pluck the bird on your lap. Keep a bucket or good-sized bag handy to collect the feathers.

Pluck either from the tail towards the head (in other words, in the opposite direction from which the feathers grow), or from head to tail. It does not matter a great deal which way you do it but if the skin is fragile the latter method is probably better. The wing feathers should be plucked out singly; if they are tough, use a pair of pliers. If you pour boiling water over the wings this will soften the skin and making plucking easier.

Drawing

Cut off the head a couple of inches from the body. Pull the neck skin down towards the body and cut off the neck.

Slit the skin from the breast upwards towards the head, making a slit just long enough to remove the crop and windpipe. Make another slit from vent to abdomen, this time just large enough to get the fingers inside the body cavity and remove the entrails. Set aside the giblets (gizzard, heart and liver). Wipe the inside well with a clean, damp cloth.

Remove the sinews of larger birds. Make a length-wise cut in the leg, just above the claw, to expose the sinews. Hook a skewer under each sinew, and pull them out one by one. Cut off the feet.

Singeing

Remove the last bits of down either by carefully holding the bird over a gas flame or singeing it with a long taper. Wipe the bird afterwards with a damp cloth.

Trussing

Do this after stuffing. Place the bird, breast down, on the working surface and fold the loose skin over the back. Fold the wing tips over the body to hold this in position. Next, turn the bird on its back, cut a slit in the skin above the vent and pull the parson's nose through.

Insert a poultry skewer into the body, just below the thigh bone, so that it comes out at the other side, through the opposite thigh. Turn the bird onto its breast again. Pass a piece of string over the wing tips, under, and then up over the ends of the skewer. Cross the string over the back of the bird.

Finally, turn the bird onto its back, loop the string around the drumsticks and parson's nose, and tie securely.

7
Large Game Birds

We find men, all over the world acting instinctively in strict accord with the intentions of nature to obtain food, the internal fuel which is the oil to feed life's warming lamp.

F. *Bishop*

106 Shooting game is not one of the oldest sports, because the first musket gun, made in Spain for the army in 1540, weighed forty pounds, and it was not until the time of Charles II that a gun – still cumbersome, very expensive and not always accurate – was used for killing birds. Shooting then became the new sport, and gradually increased in popularity.

In 1813, Colonel Peter Hawker published his classic *Instructions to Young Sportsmen* and he devoted practically all his time to his hobby of guns for game shooting. (In 1975, at the Game Fair at Chatsworth, a modern sporting gun was exhibited. The price? £27500 – including the case and 100 cartridges!)

The training of dogs for retrieving fallen birds also became fashionable. The name 'retriever' is obvious, but 'cocker' spaniels are supposed to have acquired their name from sportsmen after woodcock.

Early this century, when guns had still further improved, the landed gentry were employing many gamekeepers to breed birds and to protect them against poachers. Shooting started in August and went on through the winter, and this meant healthy employment for hundreds of people and ultimately provided food for hundreds more. But penal taxation and the spread of population has meant the gradual dissolution of big estates, and it has now become too expensive for most landowners to breed pheasants for sport.

Whether it is because sportsmen spend so much of their leisure, and find pleasure, in nature, the fields, the woods and the streams, I cannot say, but all those I have known personally have been extroverts, broad-minded (and often broad-bodied), patient and dependable. I recall seeing a particularly apt epitaph, at Southwell Minster, to William Clay (died 1775).

Here lies a sportsman, jolly, kind and free
From the cares and troubles of this world was he.
When living, his principal and greatest pride
Was to have a fowling bag swing by his side.
And in the fields and woods to labour, toil and run
In quest of game, with Pero, Cobb and gun.
But now, poor mortal, he from hence has gone
In hopes to find a joyful resurrection.

Poor mortal! I fear he won't be allowed to use a gun in the Elysian fields, nor his dogs Pero and Cobb to do any retrieving in the happy hunting grounds. Let us leave it. As Thomas Hood wrote:

What he hit is history.
What he missed is mystery.

Pheasant

If you enquire of friends which is their favourite game bird (cooked) you will find that 90 per cent will 'plump' for a plump pheasant, and usually roasted. In season from 1 October to 1 February, one bird will usually be sufficient for four servings.

Before you cook the bird however, there are several things to be done. First, you must check for age. This can be done by examining the wing feathers. If the first wing-tip feather is pointed, it is young, but as the pheasant grows older this becomes rounded and it is then best to cook the bird in liquor, as in a stew or casserole. It is usual to hang pheasant (by the neck) for four days, before plucking and removing the entrails. The neck, heart, liver and gizzard should be retained.

My friend F. H. E. (Fred) Buller, master gunsmith, dead shot and brilliant angler, warns me against yellow fat in pheasants. Remove this, he says, or there may be an unpleasant flavour. If you can't remove it without skinning the bird, well, skin it, and if you wish to roast it, replace the skin on the breast with egg, breadcrumbs and dripping well mixed.

Roast Pheasant

For young birds it is really only necessary to put a good lump of butter inside and truss them, smear butter over the outside and tie fat bacon over the breasts. Put in a hot oven (425°F, 220°C, gas mark 7). After 25 minutes, remove the bacon, baste the birds and cook another 10–15 minutes, keeping them well basted. Serve with bacon rolls, fried crumbs, game chips and bread sauce (page 175).

See photograph facing page 128.

Stuffings for Roast Pheasant

In the Victorian era, when meat was cheap, a pheasant was often stuffed with beef steak (not to be eaten with the bird). This was believed to enhance the flavour, the steak being used for another dish, or to make stock.

Stuffing for roast pheasant can of course vary from the lump of butter to the foie gras, via cream cheese with walnuts, chestnuts and peeled grapes, sausage meat and chicken's livers, breadcrumbs and suet, grated orange peel, onions and shallots and mushrooms. Even the familiar thyme and parsley stuffing is not to be despised (see the stuffing for Roast Duck 1 on page 124). Some prefer the flavour of sage, mace or nutmeg. But even the thought of a stuffed roast pheasant brings back to me the sad memory of a brace of pheasants, so well-cooked, in my house, at my table, and consumed with great gusto by my friends, whilst I, on a strict ten-day liquid diet, was allowed only a cup of cold consommé.

At one time, bread sauce (see page 175) was served with roast pheasant and brown gravy made from the giblets, the birds being 'nested' on a bed of fresh watercress, but recently chestnut purée has become popular. This can be made with chestnuts which are roasted, peeled, puréed and mixed with butter and a minced onion, but it can also be bought tinned and then only needs warming with a little butter, salt and pepper and 4–6 tablespoons of double cream to make a lovely smooth sauce.

Which recalls another memory of the day I stopped to lunch at a West Country hotel and found roast pheasant on the menu. A guest at the next table asked the waitress if they had any watercress. She stared. Then she said, 'Watercress! Ar, we has watercress, but we only sarves that at tea-toime.'

Roast pheasant is almost a 'must' for plump young birds but, curiously, one of our best known and very popular sportsmen, Wilson Stephens (former editor of the *Field*) has said that he likes 'any kind of game; anything other than roasted for choice; gently simmered in a casserole with red wine or Calvados'. I rather think Mr Stephens would approve of this recipe found in a monastery in Alcantara about 1807:

Pheasant Alcantara

Empty the pheasant and stuff with foie gras mixed with quartered truffles cooked in port wine. Cover the whole bird with port wine for three days, then take it out, put it in a covered dish and cook (in a moderate oven, 350°F, 180°C, gas mark 4, for 30–35 minutes). Meanwhile boil the marinade wine to reduce it somewhat, add 12 more medium-sized truffles, replace the pheasant in this and finish cooking.

Faisan Diable

One method is to cook and cut up the bird as in the foregoing recipe and cover with a sauce made with a teaspoon each of made mustard and Worcestershire sauce, a few drops of Tabasco sauce, a pinch of cayenne pepper and ½ pint (300ml) milk and ¼ pint (150ml) cream stirred in. This is poured over the bird and the whole contents heated up in a warm oven (325°F, 160°C, gas mark 3) for about 15 minutes.

Faisan au Verger

1 pheasant
2 sticks celery, chopped
1 onion, peeled and sliced
1 apple, peeled and sliced
salt and pepper
½pt (300ml) cider

This is a very good way of cooking an older bird. Prepare and roast it in a moderate oven (350°F, 180°C, gas mark 4) first, for about 30 minutes (it should not be overdone). Then cut the bird into eight pieces (two legs, two wings, and the breast cut into four lengthwise).

Fry the chopped celery, and sliced onion and apple. When soft, put with the bird pieces in a casserole, pour over the cider and season with salt and pepper. If necessary add sufficient water to level with the contents. Cover and cook another 10–15 minutes at the same temperature. *Serves 4.*

Pheasant à la Normande

1 plump pheasant
1½oz (40g) butter
6 medium-sized apples, peeled and sliced
cream

Prepare and truss the pheasant, brown it by turning it in a pan in the butter and set aside. In the same butter, cook the apples gently for about 5 minutes. Put half of these in a fireproof dish, set the pheasant thereon and add the rest of the apples. Spoon over some fresh cream, cover and cook in a moderate oven (350°F, 180°C, gas mark 4) for 40 minutes. *Serves 4.*

Salmis de Faisan

1 pheasant
2 tablespoons brandy
a little beef consommé

For the sauce

the pheasant carcase, giblets and trimmings
½ bottle red wine
3 shallots, chopped
2 green peppers
1 bay leaf
sprig of parsley
¼pt (150ml) Espagnole sauce (see page 174)
1oz (25g) butter

Escoffier considered pheasant salmis (an old fashioned recipe) one of the most delicate and perfect of game preparations, but claimed that over the years it had been spoiled by haphazard treatment. His instructions are to roast the pheasant in a moderate oven (350°F, 180°C, gas mark 4) for about 30 minutes (it should not be overdone), then cut it up into eight pieces (two legs, two wings, and the breast cut into four, length-wise). Put in a pan, flambé with brandy, add a little beef consommé. Then make the sauce as follows:

Put the carcase, giblets and trimmings in another pan with the red wine, chopped shallots and green peppers, a bay leaf and a sprig of parsley. Add the Espagnole sauce, cook for 10 minutes, strain, return the liquid to the pan and boil till reduced by one third. Off the heat, mix in the butter and pour over the pieces of pheasant. *Serves 4.*

Actually, this method can be applied to all feathered game.

Leaving the pheasants cooking, it might be interesting to recall that our pheasants are really hybrids between the Caucasian pheasant of the Romans and the ring-necked pheasant, which was a native of eastern China.

Grilled Pheasant

Another way is to coat the cooked serving pieces with melted butter, sprinkle them with cayenne pepper, roll in breadcrumbs, dot over a little more butter and grill until golden brown.

Pheasant cooked in this way is very good if served with the traditional accompaniments to roast pheasant, e.g., cranberry sauce (page 176), game chips, or perhaps red wine sauce (page 179).

Partridge

Partridges are highly nutritious, living mostly on foods which give them a delicate flavour. They should be hung, depending on the weather and individual taste, for from two to five days. Allow one bird per person.

They are in season from 1 September to 1 February, but at their best in October and November. They are checked for age in the same way as pheasants and can also be cooked by the same methods. The rather larger French or Red-legged partridges are, in their native country, usually browned in butter, then roasted without stuffing. The giblets are cooked in stock till tender, minced finely, seasoned, and spread on slices of fried bread. Then the birds are placed on top and sometimes served with fried aubergines. However, both the English and French species may be cooked in the same way.

Roast Partridge

2 young partridges

For the stuffing
2oz (50g) white breadcrumbs
grated rind of 1 lemon
a few crushed juniper berries
1 tablespoon chopped parsley
pinch of mixed herbs
salt and pepper
1 egg, beaten
4 fat bacon rashers

To make the stuffing, mix together the white breadcrumbs, the grated lemon rind, crushed juniper berries, chopped parsley, mixed herbs, salt and pepper. Bind with the beaten egg, stuff the birds, wrap them in fat pork and roast in a moderate oven (350°F, 180°C, gas mark 4) for an hour, basting occasionally with the frying butter.

A tablespoonful of seedless raisins could be used instead of the juniper berries. *Serves 2.*

Grilled Partridge

If the birds are very young, instead of trussing, cut them in half, length-wise, remove the pinion bones, dip in melted butter, season with salt and pepper and grill for 7 minutes, turning and basting three times. Serve with Bordelais sauce (page 174).

Partridge au Choux

4 plump partridges
6oz (175g) fat pork rashers
a little flour
2oz (50g) butter
1 onion, minced
1 hard green cabbage, about 2lb (1kg)
pepper
½pt (300ml) red wine

Being fairly small, it is best if you can cook
a brace of partridges at a time. Assuming they
are already trussed, tie some of the fat pork
over the breasts – about 2oz (50g) should be
sufficient – roll in flour and fry in hot butter.
Take the birds out of the pan. Fry the remaining fat pork with the minced onion until
crisp. Take the white cabbage, remove any
tough outer leaves and shred it, put half in
a casserole with the fried pork and onion,
pepper lightly, add the birds and the rest of
the cabbage. Pour over the red wine, cover
and bake in a slow oven (325°F, 160°C, gas
mark 3) for 1½ hours. *Serves 4.*

Partridge à Chou Rouge

This is also a good method for older birds.

4 partridges
½lb (225g) fat pork, in one piece
1 red cabbage, quartered
2oz (50g) butter, melted

Put them in a stewpan, cover with well-
seasoned stock, bring to the boil and then
simmer slowly until tender.

Meanwhile dice the fat pork (*petit salé* to
the French, belly-pork to the British and
(don't shudder) sow's udder to the Romans)
and fry in a deep pan until it begins to crisp.
In another saucepan, cook the quartered red
cabbage till soft. Take it out, drain it, cut up
and put a layer in a deep casserole dish, then
half the pork. Place the birds on this, put in
the rest of the pork then the rest of the
cabbage. Heat the pork fat, add the melted
butter and pour this over the top. Cover and
cook in a fairly hot oven (375°F, 190°C, gas
mark 5) for 30 minutes. *Serves 4.*

Grouse

As all sportsmen know, the shooting season begins with grouse on 12 August (the 'Glorious Twelfth'). Their season ends on 15 December, and during this time these fine birds are in great demand in homes and restaurants. They are usually hung for a few days and young birds are roasted or split down the back and grilled, in much the same way as pheasant. In general, a young grouse is only enough for one, but a more mature bird should be just enough for two.

Roast Grouse with Brandy Sauce

2 young grouse
butter
¼pt (150ml) brandy
½pt (300ml) cream
salt and pepper

Brown 2 young grouse in butter in a frying pan, then remove to a roasting pan, baste with more butter, cover and cook in a slow oven (325°F, 160°C, gas mark 3) for 45 minutes. Add the brandy to the butter in the frying pan, bring to the boil, add the cream slowly, stirring well. Season with salt and pepper, pour over the birds, heat up and serve. My Continental friends claim the brandy should be ignited before the cream is added. *Serves 2.*

White sauce can be substituted for the cream, but it's not, of course, quite as good as the real thing.

Grouse à la Georgienne

1 old grouse
½pt (300ml) dry white wine or cider
1 wineglass port wine
½pt (300ml) orange juice
½pt (300ml) cold tea
2oz (50g) butter
salt and pepper
½pt (300ml) Espagnole sauce (see page 174)

Put into a casserole the dry white wine, port wine, orange juice, cold tea, butter, salt and pepper. Put the trussed bird in this, cover and cook in a moderate oven (350°F, 180°C, gas mark 4) for 40 minutes. Take out the bird, stir in the Espagnole sauce, boil for 20 minutes to reduce the liquor, put back the bird for a few minutes to reheat and serve. *Serves 2.*

Grouse Spatchcock

2 plump grouse
olive oil
lemon juice
salt and pepper
butter
4 large rashers of bacon
4 slices white bread
¼pt (150ml) dry vermouth or kirsch
1 dessertspoon quince or redcurrant jelly
chopped parsley

The name 'spatch-cock' is said to have derived from the time when a cock had to be quickly 'dispatched' to make a meal. Now it appears to apply more to game birds, and grouse are very good cooked this way if the birds are young. The backbone should be broken so that the grouse can be laid and beaten flat. Professional cooks have a method of folding and pinioning the wings and legs, and skewering this way, that way and every which way, but for home consumption I think it's a waste of time. It all has to be undone again before you can eat.

'Paint' the birds with oil and lemon juice mixed, add salt and pepper and let them soak for a while. Then fry them in hot butter for a few minutes, turning to brown each side well. Remove from pan, cover and keep warm. Fry the four large (or eight small) rashers of bacon and then the bread, sliced into eight triangles, till crisp. Remove them also and keep warm. (Most of the fat will have been absorbed by the bread.) Add to the remainder the dry vermouth (or kirsch), boil up and add the jelly. Stir till melted. Arrange the bread and bacon on a serving dish, put the birds on top and pour over the gravy. Garnish with chopped parsley. *Serves 2.*

With older birds it is best to stick to stews or casseroles, or at least to poach them.

Swedish Grouse

4 grouse
a little dripping
1 carrot, sliced
1 onion, sliced
salt and pepper
a few crushed juniper berries
¼pt (150ml) red wine
½pt (300ml) stock or bouillon
1 tablespoon redcurrant jelly
1 tablespoon brandy
2 tablespoons cornflour
¼pt (150ml) cream

Although I have never been to Sweden, I have entertained friends from that country and English friends of mine have been to Sweden and come back with the occasional recipe. This is one of the most successful.

Clean and truss the birds, brown them all over in hot fat and put in a casserole. Add the sliced carrot and onion, salt, pepper and crushed juniper berries. Pour in the red wine and stock or bouillon. Cover and cook them in a slow oven for an hour. Take out the birds, keep them hot and make a sauce of the liquid by adding a tablespoon of redcurrant jelly and a tablespoonful of brandy. Dissolve the cornflour in a little water, add to the sauce and cook for about 5 minutes to thicken, stir in the cream and fold smoothly into the sauce. *Serves 4.*

Before we forget grouse, let us remember a sportsman of the past. At Bewcastle, near Carlisle, a tombstone pays a tribute to one Jonathan Telford: 'The deceased was one of the best grouse-shooters in the North of England. In the time of his shooting he bagged fifty-nine grouse in seven double shots.'

Capercailzie

The capercailzie, a member of the grouse family and the largest game bird, is supposed to be of Swedish origin and is not to be found 'south of the border'. In Scotland its habitat is chiefly in or around the forests of conifers, because it is very partial to pine shoots, from the consumption of which it acquires a peculiar turpentine-like flavour.

In season from 20 August till 10 December, capercailzie should be hung for six to seven days.

One of my young Scottish friends who, like his compatriots, has a pawky sense of humour, solemnly advised me that, should I ever shoot a capercailzie, I must cover it reverently, then make all speed to report to the nearest gamekeeper, ghillie, stalker, or Forestry Commission warden, so that a funeral service could be arranged without delay.

Naturally, I was surprised more than somewhat by this information, but, he went on gravely:

The capercailzie is not edible and has no protection in law, therefore we feel that its death is unwarranted and we must atone by giving it reverent obsequies. The procession will be led by the local Orpheus choir chanting the 'Capercailzie Requiem'. You and a friend will follow carrying the bird shoulder high on a hurdle, then lower it silently into the grave (which you have prepared while waiting for arrangements to be made) and the pipers of the Black Watch will play the lament, 'Flowers of the Forest'. The warden (or whoever is in charge) will pronounce *Requiescat in pace* and you will be left to fill in the grave.

And what, I asked, is the 'Capercailzie Requiem'? My young friend took up his accordion and sang softly and lugubriously:

When I die carry me shoulder high,
To a grave in the glen where I want to lie.
Cover my grave with bracken and heather.
A funeral song for bird of brown feather.
In this dear land – the end of my tether
When I die!

Casseroled Capercailzie

After that, who could think of eating a capercailzie? But, there are times when needs must. An old cookery book tells you to first take out the crop (probably pine shoots), and hang the bird in a current of air for two or three weeks. Pluck it, draw it and truss it. Soak it for ten hours in milk, another ten hours in vinegar and a further ten hours in a marinade of red wine with crushed garlic and juniper berries. Take out the bird, dry and flour it, put in a casserole with oil already heated, turn it around to brown. Pour over the marinade, add a pint (600ml) of stock, salt and pepper and cook slowly for 2½ hours, adding redcurrant jelly when serving. And *requiescat in pace*!

Blackcock

This is a species of grouse and can be cooked in the same way, but should be well hung. The flesh (as in most of the small game birds) tends to be dry. It is therefore wise to put butter inside, fat bacon outside, and baste often. Roast in a moderately hot oven (375°F, 190°C, gas mark 5) for 45–60 minutes depending on size. Older birds are best marinated for twenty-four hours before cooking.

Ptarmigan

Sometimes called the white grouse, it should be cooked like Blackcock, but very old birds, even when marinated, tend to have rather a bitter flavour. Serve with gravy, bread sauce (see page 175) and fried crumbs.

8

Small Game Birds

When I demanded of my friend
What viands he preferred,
He quoth 'A large cold bottle and
a small hot bird!'

Eugene Field

Woodcock

The woodcock, like the capercailzie, is said to have been originally an immigrant from Scandinavia, whence it crossed the North Sea to find a new home in the beautiful forest areas of Scotland. It is now common in suitable habitats throughout the British islands. It is in season between 1 October and 31 January but at its best in November and December. An average woodcock should be sufficient for one person.

Among chefs, opinion seems to be divided, some refusing to cook any birds which have been bruised or damaged, some declaring they should be cooked as fresh as possible, others recommending that they be hung for at least three days. All agree that they should not be drawn (except that the gizzard should be removed), their alimentary canal being one single gut or trail which becomes liquified by heat. They must on no account be overcooked, 10–15 minutes in a hot oven (425°F, 220°C, gas mark 7) usually being sufficient. Professional chefs also have a peculiar idea of skinning the head (after taking out the eyes) and tucking it back under the bird, the beak acting as a skewer. Amateur cooks among my friends like the birds drawn and trussed like any other fowl.

Boiled Woodcock or Snipe

The Accomplish't Lady's Delight gives the following recipe:

Boyl them either in strong broath, or in water and salt, and being boyled, take out the Guts, and chop them small with the Liver, put to it some crumbs or grated white-bread, a little Cock-broath, and some large Mace; stew them together with some Gravy, then dissolve the Yolks of two Eggs in some wine-vinegar, and a little grated Nutmeg, and when you are ready to Dish it, put in the Eggs, and stir it among the Sauce with a little butter; Dish them on Sippets, and run the Sauce over them with some beaten butter and capers, a Lemon minced small, Barberries or whole pickled Grapes.

Roast Woodcock

1 woodcock per person
butter
1 fat bacon rasher for each bird
1 slice white bread for each bird
slices of lemon

Rub the birds over with butter and place a rasher of fat bacon over each breast. Put on a grid in a baking dish with croûtons of fried bread underneath to catch the drippings, cover and cook in a preheated hot oven (425°F, 220°C, gas mark 7) for 10–15 minutes. Serve them split in two length-ways on croûtons with slices of lemon.

Some cooks sauté the intestines, add salt and pepper, a few drops of lemon juice, mix well and spread on the croûtons under the birds.

Woodcock Casserole

1 woodcock per person
the intestines
¼pt (150ml) stock
1 glass red wine
6 peppercorns
1 clove of garlic, minced
bouquet garni
butter
flour

Prepare, roast and halve as in the preceding recipe. While cooking, mince and mix the intestines and simmer gently with the stock, red wine, peppercorns, garlic and *bouquet garni*. Thicken with a little butter and flour mixed to a paste. Strain and pour over the birds.

Some prefer white wine and nutmeg to red wine and peppercorns, and a little mustard instead of garlic. Added minced lamb's liver and bacon will eke out the dish, if necessary.

Snipe

120 Although snipe is in season in Britain from
12 August to 31 January, it is at its best in
the cold winter months. Hang for 3–4 days.
Allow one or two per person, depending on
the size of the bird.

Plover

Only golden plovers may be shot in Britain,
between 1 September and 31 January, all
others being protected. They are cooked
undrawn, like snipe and woodcock, and
generally roasted. Allow one bird per person.

Italian Snipe

Snipe are cooked very much in the same way
as woodcock, but in Italy and along the
Mediterranean, the birds are prepared as
beforementioned, then browned in hot olive
oil and cooked, casserole fashion, in a sauce
made with tomatoes (peeled and seeded),
chopped stoned olives, crushed garlic, cayenne
pepper, salt, and meat stock. After cooking
for 30 minutes add a glass of red wine. Serve
on fried bread croûtons.

Pluvier aux Olives

Stone some olives, stuff them with pimentoes
and put a few in each plover. Wrap each bird
in bacon, put in a well buttered fireproof dish
and roast in a moderate oven (350°F, 180°C,
gas mark 4) for 20 minutes, keeping well
basted. Serve on croûtons.

Quail

While one seldom, if ever, finds quail for sale in the shops and wildfowlers mostly turn their guns to bigger birds, one occasionally sees quail (and quail eggs) advertised. They are now being bred commercially. As they are small birds, one would need two birds per person. They should be eaten as soon as possible after killing.

Caille à la Dauphine

French chefs nearly always wrap each little quail in a buttered vine leaf and a thin slice of bacon.

2 quail per person
8 buttered vine leaves
4oz (100g) thin bacon rashers
1pt (600ml) shelled green peas
1 lettuce
few sprigs of mint

For this recipe, prepare the birds this way and roast, covered, in a hot oven (425°F, 210°C, gas mark 7) for 10 minutes. Remove the bacon and vine leaves. Cook the shelled green peas with the washed leaves of a lettuce and a few sprigs of mint in salted water until just tender. Strain. Remove the mint, and purée the peas in a liquidizer.

Line a fireproof serving dish with very thin slices of fat bacon, pour in the purée, and plunge the birds in this, but leave the breasts exposed. Put back in the oven for 10 minutes and serve, preferably with new potatoes. *Serves 4.*

Quail with Apple

2 quail, ready for cooking
olive oil
butter
1 slice of white bread
1 small, firm apple, thickly sliced
freshly ground black pepper

Brush the birds with olive oil, then roast in a hot oven (425°F, 210°C, gas mark 7) for about 10 minutes. Meanwhile fry the bread in butter until golden brown. Drain and set aside. Sauté the apple pieces in butter also until golden, but not mushy. Pepper lightly and cover until required.

When the quail are cooked, place them on the *croûte,* and arrange the apple pieces around them. A good sauce to accompany this would be that given for Roast Widgeon, on page 127.

See photograph facing page 129.

Landrail

This plump, delicate small bird commonly called the corncrake, and now virtually extinct in England, is in season only from 12 August to mid-September, and is usually roasted, buttered inside and out and frequently basted, as it is rather dry. Put some minced parsley, a chopped shallot, salt and pepper with the butter inside each bird. Roast in a fairly hot oven (400°F, 200°C, gas mark 6) for about 25 minutes and serve with brown gravy.

Alexis Soyer, famous chef of the Reform Club, was renowned for his humanity. Curiously, his love for his fellow men did not extend to fish and fowl, because there is a record of a gargantuan banquet he arranged for the Lord Mayor of York, who was entertaining Prince Albert in the Guildhall of that historic city. The meal included turtles' heads, grouse, pheasant and 'the choicest parts of 100 snipe and 72 larks'.

9
Wild Fowl

Let us be thankful for the good, beauty
and benison of food.
Let us join chiming vowel with vowel to
rhapsodize fish, flesh and fowl.

Louis Untermeyer

124 My friend Pete Thomas, well known as an adept angler, is an equally efficient wildfowler, and more than one wild duck or goose from his bag has come my way. They can be shot between 1 September and 31 January (under certain conditions, 28 February). It must be cooked within twenty-four hours of shooting. Mallard is the largest and best-known variety. Allow one of these for two to three people.

Wild duck should be plucked, drawn and trussed in the same way as a domestic bird, Wild fowl have extremely dry flesh and those coming from coastal areas can also have a fishy flavour. It is therefore advisable to put the bird in a large pan of cold salted water, bring to the boil, then let it simmer for 15 to 20 minutes. Remove the bird and wash it, and dry it inside and out.

Roast Duck 1

1 wild duck

For the stuffing
duck giblets
breadcrumbs
4oz (100g) softened butter
chopped parsley
pinch of thyme
pepper and salt
fat bacon rashers

Stew the giblets until soft, mince, add an equal quantity of breadcrumbs, the softened butter, chopped parsley, a pinch of thyme, pepper and salt. Stuff the bird with this, rub more butter over the skin of the duck, cover the breast with fat bacon and roast in a moderate oven (350°F, 180°C, gas mark 4) for about 1 hour (according to size), basting frequently. Take off the pork 10 minutes before removing the duck from the oven, baste again and serve with apple sauce (page 175) or sauerkraut.

Roast Duck 2

1 wild duck
3 tablespoons fat
3 tablespoons flour

For the stuffing
3 cups hot mashed potatoes
1 cup breadcrumbs
1 onion, grated
½ cup chopped salt pork
1 teaspoon powdered sage
salt and pepper
1 egg, beaten

Rub the bird over with seasoned fat. To make the stuffing, mix the hot mashed potatoes with the breadcrumbs, grated onion, chopped pork, powdered sage, salt and pepper. Bind with the beaten egg. Fill the duck, close the opening with a skewer and truss. Mix the 3 tablespoons of fat and flour together and spread this thickly over the breast of the bird. Cook in a slow oven (300°F, 150°C, gas mark 2), allowing 20–25 minutes per pound. Ten minutes before the end, remove the 'crust' and baste the bird, browning the breast.

Canard Candide

If instead of 1 large duck you have 2 small ones, it is best to cook them this way.

2 small wild duck
seasoned flour
butter or oil for frying
1 large onion, minced
2 tablespoons tomato purée
2 tablespoons lemon juice
2 teaspoons powdered cardamon
1 cup chopped nuts (walnut, hazelnut or pecan)
2 cups cider

Cut the duck into serving pieces, roll in seasoned flour, fry in oil or butter till golden brown, then turn down the heat and cook very slowly, turning occasionally.

In another pan, fry the large minced onion for a few minutes, add the tomato sauce and lemon juice, cardamon, chopped nuts and cider. Cook until the onion is soft. Arrange the birds on a hot dish and spoon the sauce over. *Serves 4.*

An equally delectable alternative to the tomato sauce, lemon juice, cardamon, nuts and cider is chopped celery and apples, cooked with the onion in ¼ pint (150ml) of burgundy and seasoned with freshly ground black pepper.

Canard Flambé à l'Eau de Vie

2 small wild duck
seasoned flour
butter for frying
1 clove garlic, minced
1 carrot, sliced thinly
salt and pepper
¼pt (150ml) brandy
2 tablespoons flour
¼pt (150ml) dry white wine

Make this *de luxe* dish by first frying the pieces as described in the preceding recipe. Remove them, and in the butter sauté the garlic and carrot for a few minutes. Replace the duck and season with salt and pepper. Pour over the brandy and set it alight. When the flame has died down, sprinkle over the flour to absorb the fat, add the wine, slightly warmed, cover and simmer for 20 minutes. *Serves 4.*

This is good accompanied by fried mushrooms. It can be prepared the day before required and reheated.

Canard Épicé

1 wild duck
2 chopped shallots
2 cloves
1 tablespoon green peppercorns
1pt (600ml) stock
salt and pepper

For the marinade

¼pt (150ml) olive oil
¼pt (150ml) red wine
1 teaspoon allspice
1 bay leaf
salt and pepper

Here is another good way – this time a French one – of dealing with a bird no longer in the first flush of youth. Truss as for roasting. Make a marinade with the olive oil, red wine, allspice, bay leaf, salt and pepper. Marinade the duck in this for some hours, turning from time to time. Next, roast in a pan, with the marinade, in a fairly hot oven (400°F, 200°C, gas mark 6) for half an hour, basting frequently. Take the bird out, set aside to cool, then cut into joints. Put the marinade in a stewpan with the shallots, cloves, green peppercorns, stock, salt and pepper. Boil up, simmer for 15 minutes, add the duck pieces, cook a further 15 minutes and serve. *Serves 2–3.*

Morena Duck

This is really a recipe for a domestic duck, popular along the Mediterranean coast, but it is equally good with a prepared wild duck.

1 wild duck
olive oil for frying
paprika
1 onion, minced
1 clove garlic, crushed
1 tomato, peeled, seeded and sliced
1 tablespoon flour
½pt (300ml) chicken stock
¼pt (150ml) Madeira
2 tablespoons chopped olives

Cut the bird into convenient serving pieces, brown them in olive oil, put in a casserole and sprinkle well with paprika.

Add a little more oil to the frying pan, sauté the minced onion, garlic and sliced tomato for a few minutes. Mix the tablespoon of flour with a little water, add the chicken stock and Madeira, and add this gradually to the pan. Simmer until it thickens; finally, mix in the chopped olives, pour over the duck, cover and cook in a moderate oven (350°F, 180°C, gas mark 4) for 1 hour. *Serves 2–3.*

Widgeon and Teal

Some gourmets consider widgeon, a variety of wild duck, to have a better flavour than the mallard. They advocate hanging for about three days before plucking and drawing and then trussing with the feet still on (laid alongside the breast) the neck removed close to the body, leaving as much outside skin as possible to draw over and fix to the back.

Teal is another waterfowl so similar to the widgeon that it is treated and cooked in much the same way. Allow one bird per serving.

Roast Widgeon

2–3 widgeon
pork fat or bacon
butter for roasting
a little flour
squeeze of lemon juice

For the sauce

2 onions, minced
a little butter
1 dessertspoon flour
pinch of cayenne pepper
$\frac{3}{4}$pt (450ml) stock
1 glass port wine
1 tablespoon redcurrant jelly

Roast the birds without any stuffing, but cover the breast with pork fat or bacon and baste frequently while roasting for about 30 minutes in a fairly hot oven (400°F, 200°C, gas mark 6). Leave the bird rather under than overdone.

After the fat is removed, sprinkle the breast with flour and return the bird to the oven for a final 5 minutes. Sprinkle with lemon juice and serve on watercress.

Make a good sauce to accompany the roast widgeon by frying the minced onions in a little butter, adding the flour and pinch of cayenne pepper to the stock and port wine. Blend in the redcurrant jelly, simmer for about 15 minutes and serve with the birds. *Serves 4.*

The author of *The Accomplish't Lady's Delight* thought differently. This is her recipe:

Parboyl your widgeons and then stick whole cloves in their breasts, put into their bellies a little winter savoury or Parsley; boyl them in a pipkin by themselves, thicken with toastes, season with verjuice, sugar and a little pepper; garnish your dish with barberries and pruans and so serve them.

On only one occasion have I been given widgeon for dinner, and I have no recollection of what it tasted like, being condemned to sit beside a sunny, funny, punny dinner companion, with a joke for every course, and at the serving of this one he turned to me and solemnly remarked, ''Tis now the widgeon hour of night.'

Wild Goose

Probably because of the vast distances flown by wild geese, they carry no superfluous fat and, like wild ducks, their flesh is very, very dry and needs a lot of 'greasing' to make it succulent. Some recommend hanging for about three weeks, but one would be average. Only young birds are good to eat, so make sure your specimen has legs of a fresh, bright colour, and a pliable underbill.

Generally, geese are roasted, in the same way as wild duck, but with added fat.

In the days of lengthy menus – and appetites – diners were allocated half a goose each. These were, of course, mostly the fat domestic breeds. In one of Surtees's books there is a vivid description of a splendid meal:

For people who are fond of goose (and who is not?) a greater treat could not be devised. They sat down to dine . . . in the fairest and most equitable way imaginable, for instead of a favoured few getting the breast and tit-bits, leaving nothing but gristly drumsticks for late-comers, each man had his own half of goose and could take whatever part he liked first, without eating in haste for fear that the next favoured cut would be gone, ere he could get at it again.

Roast Pheasant
See page 107 for recipe

Oie à Cidre

1 goose
fat for roasting
1 orange, quartered
1 apple, quartered
4oz (100g) butter
pork fat
½pt (300ml) stock
good ½pt (300ml) dry cider
1oz (25g) butter, seasoned with salt and
  freshly ground black pepper

Prepare for roasting like a duck, then put the quartered orange and apple and the butter inside. Secure the opening with a small skewer. Tie slices of fat pork round the goose, put it in a roasting tin, breast down, pour in the stock (made by stewing the giblets with onion, salt and pepper and herbs) and cider, cover and cook in a pre-heated hot oven (400°F, 200°C, gas mark 6) for 30 minutes. Baste, add more cider and salt and pepper, reduce the heat to 300°F, 150°C, gas mark 2 and continue cooking, basting occasionally, for 1½ hours, then turn the bird over, take off the pork fat from the breast, baste again and rub with the seasoned butter. Cover the pan and cook for another 30 minutes, then remove the cover, baste yet again, turn up the heat and put back long enough to brown the breast.

Serve with red cabbage, cooked with apples in cider.

An alternative stuffing of celery, onions and sage, with salt, pepper and plenty of butter can be used, or red wine instead of cider. In that case serve with braised leeks.

The French, who love a flambé, would, just before serving, pour over the breast a wine-glass of warmed brandy and set it alight.

It would seem that our ancestors were partial to goose pie, and in the *Newcastle Chronicle* of 6 January 1770, it was reported:

Monday last was brought from Howick to Berwick to be shipped to London from Sir Henry Grey-Bart, a pie, the contents were as follows:
4 Wild Geese, 4 Wild Ducks, 2 Turkies, 4 Partridges, 6 Snipes, 2 Woodcocks, 2 Curlews, 7 Blackbirds, 6 Pigeons, 2 Rabbits, 20lbs Butter and 2 Bushells of Flour.

It was near 9 ft at circumference and weighed about 12 stones.

However, it wasn't only in Northumberland that prodigious pies were produced. Yorkshire people will tell you of a famous recipe which appeared in a cookery book in 1700 and has turned up since at intervals from 1769 to 1927. Here it is:

Quail with Apple
See page 121 for recipe

Yorkshire Goose Pie

Take a large fat goose; split it down the back, take all the bones out. Bone a turkey the same way, also two ducks. Season them very well with pepper and salt, also six woodcocks; lay the goose down on a clean dish with the skin side down, and lay the turkey into the goose with the skin down. Have ready a large hare cleaned well, cut in pieces and stewed in the oven, with a pound of butter, a quarter of an ounce of mace beat fine, the same of white pepper and salt to your taste, till the meat will leave the bones and skim the butter off the gravy; pick the meat clean and beat it in a marble mortar very fine, with the butter you took off and lay it in the turkey. Take 24lb of the finest flour, six lb of butter and half-a-pound of fresh rendered suet; make the paste pretty thick and raise the pie oval, roll out a lump of paste and cut it in vine leaves or what form you please; rub the pie with yolks of eggs and put your ornaments on the walls; then turn the hare, turkey and goose upside down and lay them in your pie with the ducks at each end and the woodcocks on the sides. Make your lid pretty thick and put it on; you may lay flowers or the shape of flowers in paste on your lid and make a hole in the middle of the lid; the walls of the pie are to be one inch and a-half higher than the lid; then rub it all over with the yolks of eggs and bind it round with three-fold paper, and lay the same over the top; it will take four hours baking in a brown-bread oven; when it comes out melt two pounds of butter in the gravy that comes from the hare and pour it hot in the pie through a turn-dish; close it up well and let it be eight or ten days before you cut it.

The Americans have a poor opinion of wild geese for the table. None of my friends has ever cooked one, the general opinion being that any which get shot are very old and therefore tough. Maybe this is because the Canada Goose is quite different from the Grey Goose of Great Britain. However, a brief reference in an American cookery book merely says, 'stuff with celery leaves and cook for three or four hours'.

Summing up, I would cook a wild goose like a wild duck, allowing extra time according to the size, but when in doubt as to age and toughness, cut it up, simmer till tender and use in minces, casseroles or game pies.

10

Pigeons and Rooks

Now good digestion wait on appetite
and health on both

Macbeth

Pigeons

It used to be said in rural areas that 'January brings the snow – and the wood pigeons.' And farmers feared for the clover and gardeners for their brussel sprouts. 'Shoots' were organized as soon as possible, although as surplus dead birds fetched only a few pence, and time and cartridges cost money, it was mostly those who regarded pigeon-shooting as sport who were willing to turn out.

In recent years, pigeons seem to have deserted clover for oil-seed rape, which has arrived on the farming scene for spring and winter sowing and on which the pigeons have become 'hooked'. Pigeons fetch a good price in the export market, which is probably why one seldom sees them for sale in poultry shops. They are also being bought for canning. Nevertheless, kind friends occasionally arrive with a full bag and expect to leave with a full stomach.

It is best to cook pigeons fresh. They should never be hung like game birds, but they can be kept for a day or two if the crops are emptied at once. They are fairly easy to pluck, but if you have a considerable number, cut along the breast bone with a sharp knife, peel back the skin and remove, complete with the feathers.

Roast Pigeon 1

Just put the birds in a greased baking tin, cover with fat pork slices and roast in a fairly hot oven (400°F, 200°C, gas mark 6) for 15–20 minutes. Allow 1 bird per person.

In recent years, they have been served with cranberry sauce (see page 176).

Roast Pigeon 2

3 pigeons
a little flour
salt and pepper
1 cup breadcrumbs
the yolks of 2 hard-boiled eggs
pinch of nutmeg
2 drops Tabasco
a little softened butter

Prepare as above, then after removing both back and breast bones, flatten the birds on a floured board and season with salt and pepper. Mix the breadcrumbs with the hard-boiled egg yolks, nutmeg, Tabasco sauce and enough butter to bind into a paste. Spread this over the birds and roast in a moderate oven (350°F, 180°C, gas mark 4) for about 30 minutes. *Serves 3–4.*

Pigeon en Escabèche

If the pigeons are older, they are very good cooked in the following way:

4 pigeons
½pt (300ml) white wine vinegar
¼pt (150ml) white wine
½ lemon, sliced
2oz (50g) green pepper, sliced
bouquet garni
5 green peppercorns
salt and pepper
¾pt (450ml) chicken broth
½oz (12g) powdered gelatine

Place the birds (whole) in a casserole with the white wine vinegar, white wine, sliced lemon and green pepper, *bouquet garni*, green peppercorns, salt and pepper and chicken stock and cook slowly for 2 hours. Add the powdered gelatine, put the whole lot into a suitable serving dish and chill until set. Garnish with slices of lemon and cucumber.

Stewed Pigeon

4 pigeons
oil for frying
1 pt (600ml) stock
1 glass red wine
1 onion, sliced
1 clove
4 peppercorns
bouquet garni
1 tablespoon tomato purée
salt and pepper
a little butter
a little flour

Cut each pigeon into 4 pieces, brown in oil, put into a pan with the stock, red wine, sliced onion, clove, peppercorns, *bouquet garni* and tomato purée, salt and pepper. Boil up and then simmer until tender, strain, thicken the liquor with a little flour mixed to a paste with softened butter. *Serves 4.*

Grilled or Fried Pigeon

This is only for young birds. They can, of course, be fried in butter instead of cooked under the grill.

Flatten the boned birds on a floured board as for roasting, brush over with melted butter, season with salt and pepper and grill, turning and adding a little butter occasionally.

Pigeon Pie 1

Pigeon pie is a classic, although recipes do vary. The great Escoffier advises, rather briefly: 'Line a pie-dish with thin slices of beef, put in the pigeons, quartered, with sliced hard-boiled egg, salt and black pepper. Half-fill the dish with good meat stock, cover with puff pastry and bake.'

Pigeon Pie 2

134   This is a more sumptuous production than that of Escoffier's, on the previous page.

4 pigeons
butter
½lb (225g) cubed fillet of beef
4oz (100g) chopped fat pork
2 tablespoons chopped parsley
grated rind of 1 lemon
stock
puff (or shortcrust) pastry
1 egg, beaten

For the marinade

¼pt (150ml) olive oil
¼pt (150ml) port wine
6 crushed juniper berries
6 peppercorns

First, make a marinade by mixing together the olive oil and port wine, crushed juniper berries and peppercorns. Cut the pigeons in half and remove the back and breast bones. Let them marinade for twenty-four hours, turning occasionally, then take them out, drain, dry and brown in butter. Lay them in a buttered pie dish, around a pie 'rose' (to let out steam), filling spaces with cubes of fillet of beef and some chopped fat pork. Scatter over the chopped parsley and the grated lemon rind. Strain the marinade, add sufficient stock to just drown the birds and cover with puff pastry. Decorate with the trimmings and brush over with beaten egg. Put in a pre-heated moderate oven (350°F, 180°C, gas mark 4) for 20 minutes, lower the heat to 300°F, 150°C, gas mark 2 and cook for 2 hours. If the pastry begins to brown too soon, cover with a double layer of moistened greaseproof paper.

Pigeon à la Française

This is the way our French friends use very young pigeons.

1 pigeon per person
1 rasher of bacon for each
½pt (300ml) chicken stock
chopped chives
1 teaspoon sugar
pinch of salt

For the stuffing, for each bird
the pigeon liver, finely minced
parsley
breadcrumbs
salt and pepper
beaten egg

Clean the birds and stuff them with a mixture of the minced livers, parsley, breadcrumbs, salt and pepper, bound with beaten egg.

Then truss the bird(s), cover each one with a rasher of bacon and pack into a saucepan with the chicken stock, chopped chives, sugar and a pinch of salt. Then stew them, very gently, for 30 minutes and serve with sautéd mushrooms.

Hertfordshire Pigeon Casserole

4 pigeons
seasoned flour
oil for frying
2 cloves garlic, crushed
2 onions, finely chopped
1 green pepper, thinly sliced
bouquet garni
about 1pt (600ml) stock
glass of white wine
4oz (100g) bacon
3 sticks celery
4oz (100g) mushrooms
handful of sultanas or raisins
2 teaspoons paprika
1 tablespoon redcurrant jelly

Prepare and truss the pigeons and soak them in salted water for 30 minutes. Dry, roll in seasoned flour and fry in oil, turning them to brown all over. Put them in a casserole with the crushed garlic and onions, green pepper, *bouquet garni*, ½ pint (300ml) of stock and the glass of white wine. Cover and cook for an hour. Chop the bacon, celery and mushrooms and sauté them in the oil for a few minutes. Add to the casserole with the sultanas or raisins, paprika and redcurrant jelly. Add sufficient stock to cover the birds. Cook for a further 45 minutes. Serve with boiled rice. *Serves 4.*

Pigeon Pudding

This is made like pigeon pie except that it is boiled in a basin lined and covered with suet crust.

Note: Recipes for pigeons are equally applicable to all species including the collared dove, recently removed from the list of protected species.

Rook Pie

An old emergency meal, but seldom, if ever, made these days. If adult rooks should invade your larder, remove skins, complete with feathers, and the back and breast bones. Cook them like elderly pigeons and bake them in a pie. Young rooks, shot on leaving the nests, are tender enough.

11

Venison

There is an inherent spirit for hunting
in human nature, as scarce any inhi-
bitions can restrain.

Gilbert White

138 According to history even the inmates of monasteries were not above taking part in the chase when opportunity offered. Indeed, Henry Hallam (1777–1859) tells us that the abbot of the monastery of St Denis represented to Charlemagne that the flesh of hunted animals was salutary for sick monks and, besides, their skins would serve to bind the books in the library.

Also, in 1321, the Archbishop of York always travelled with a retinue of about 200 persons (maintained at the expense of the abbeys along the route) and hunted with a pack of hounds from parish to parish.

Of course, one has to remember that these were the days before cattle-breeding had grown. Pastures were limited in size and it was impossible to feed all the stock during the winter months. So cattle were slaughtered and the meat salted down for winter provision. It was therefore understandable that a change of diet was welcome and, despite the threat of capital punishment for poaching, many a stag or wild boar was despatched and devoured with relish.

In the years following the Norman invasion and up to the sixteenth century, England still had many forests like those of Knaresborough and Galtres in Yorkshire. There is a story dating from 1351 of a Woodward (game-keeper) whose duty was to 'preserve the King's wild game and arrest poachers'. He was attacked by deer-thieves, who put out his eyes and cut off his tongue and fingers. The king gave him a pension of threepence a day (the wage of a full-time forester was then fourpence) and twenty-seven years later he was still receiving it. It has been said that some of the forest officers were not above running a medieval protection racket.

In his *Natural history of Selborne*, Gilbert White tells of how Queen Anne, on a journey to Portsmouth, sat on a bank by the road to Liphook and saw 'with great complacency and satisfaction the whole herd of red deer brought by the keepers along the vale before her, consisting then of about five hundred head'.

Unfortunately, the herd was decimated, presumably by poachers, until an order was issued to take the remaining deer alive and transfer them to Windsor Forest. Previously, local depredators had watched the herd, following any hind to see where it dropped a calf and preventing the latter's escape by mutilating its feet, although leaving it until it was fat enough to be worth killing. White tells us:

Some fellows suspecting that a calf new-fallen was deposited in a certain spot of thick fern, went with a lurcher to surprise it, when the parent hind rushed out of the brake and taking a vast spring with all her feet close together, pitched upon the neck of the dog and broke it short in two.

Despite the fact that England is now one of the most densely populated and highly industrialized countries in the world, it seems paradoxical to find that deer are increasing in numbers; at least six species are occasionally found roaming around the countryside. Of these, only the large Red deer and the graceful Roe deer are really natives. The Fallow deer was imported from Rome some hundreds of years ago, and it is, perhaps, the most familiar, since it is the species usually found in enclosed parks, although there is now a considerable wild population.

Two Acts of Parliament protect deer in this country. They are the Deer Act 1963, creating close seasons and forbidding the use of certain devices, and the Theft Act 1968, restricting its protection to deer in enclosed lands. The close season is from 1 May to 31 July and from 1 March to 31 October for Red, Fallow and Sika deer. For Roe deer it is only 1 March to 31 October. In addition to these close seasons, it is illegal to take or wilfully kill any deer of any species whatever during the night – that is, from the first hour after sunset to the commencement of the last hour before sunrise – but a new Act is now under consideration.

And, please note, a person suspected of unlawfully taking or killing a deer *can be arrested by anyone*.

Recently we have had the case of a poacher who trained his ugly great brute of a dog to pull down deer, mostly from the herd at Woburn Abbey, thus enabling his master to butcher them. The man confessed to disposing of over eighty stags and hinds, which apparently helped to stock up many a freezer.

It is due to the foresight and pertinacity of an earlier Duke of Bedford of Woburn Abbey that we have in England the Père David deer. In the middle of the nineteenth century, nobody in this country had ever heard of these rather peculiar animals, which have antlers like the well-known variety of stags, but hooves which resemble those of cows, and tails like those of donkeys. It had even been said that the necks were camels' necks. Both the stag and the hind have antlers.

A Franciscan missionary, Father David, who was stationed in China and who was deeply interested in natural history, heard stories of some rare deer in the grounds of the Emperor's palace, but they were so carefully guarded that it was impossible for any foreigners even to see them. However, with patience and probably by means of bribes to the guards, he did obtain some skins, which he sent to the

Museum of Natural History in Paris. The officers there entered into negotiations with the Chinese authorities, as a result of which a few of the deer were released to zoos in Europe, including one pair for the Duke of Bedford's private zoo at Woburn. They were thereafter known as the Père David deer. Not long after this the Yangtze River overflowed, causing serious floods, and this was followed by the Boxer rebellion. The deer escaped from the palace, only to be seized and eaten by the people. Thus, these deer became extinct in their homeland of China. The Duke of Bedford, realizing that the whole species might perish, set about collecting the odd specimens from various zoos, until he had quite a large herd of healthy animals. Then he donated pairs to various zoos and quite a number to Whipsnade.

The Muntjak deer, brought to Woburn early this century, is also from China, but it is very small. Some controversy exists as to whether it should be treated as a pet or a wild creature. The fact is that many are running wild in the countryside, but whence they came no one seems to know. There are many other rare species in Woburn, including the Rusa and Japanese Sika deer.

Unfortunately, unless one has contacts with those responsible for deer herds, it is not easy to obtain venison. Recently, however, the Highlands and Islands Development Board of Scotland have sponsored a commercial deer farm at Morven (in Argyllshire) where hundreds of Red deer will be brought. It has been reported that they are asking landowners to co-operate by leasing land for study and experiment. It is hoped that, in about four years, there will be at least 400 hinds, estimated to produce 350 calves every year. The Board expect to establish a thriving export trade and, with refrigerator containers to assist transport, the time may come when venison will replace beef for the Sunday joint in Great Britain.

In my schooldays, my father received annually a haunch or saddle of venison from the local squire, presumably because the hunt often went across his fields. I remember too, how, every year, my mother's maid-of-all-work would say, 'I ain't a goin' to eat that stuff,' and my mother would say soothingly, 'All right, Lizzie, you can fry up the rest of that meat in the safe.' So Lizzie had her fried fillet (which was a slice of the haunch) and ate it with hearty enjoyment, while the family attacked the joint.

But a day came when a hunted stag tried to leap over a hedge just in front of me as I cycled home from school. It crash-landed on a spiked iron fence surrounding an electric transformer, the sharp spikes piercing its soft breast. It was soon surrounded by huntsmen and huntswomen but there it had to stay in agony until someone could be summoned to cut its throat. I shall never forget the look in its eyes.

The meat of the Red deer, which is mostly found in the Scottish Highlands, is lean, with rather a strong flavour, which is why it should be well hung.

The Roe deer are found in woodlands. These are much smaller than Red deer and the meat is more tender and does not need hanging quite so long.

Escoffier claimed that the meat of Red deer and Fallow deer is far superior to that of Roebuck. Red deer, he said, has a little more flavour, but for delicacy and tenderness, the Fallow deer has no equal.

Although some cooks claim that the meat of a very young deer can be cooked right away, it is generally thought preferable (because of its somewhat gamey flavour) to hang the joint for two or three weeks in a dry but airy place, rubbing it dry night and morning, and then to marinade for a couple of days (see page 141 for marinade ingredients), having first interlarded it. If you don't possess a larding needle, take a sharp knife, make slits under the outer skin and insert thin slices of pork fat.

The very thought of roast venison recalls Oliver Goldsmith's tribute to Lord Clare:

Thanks, my Lord, for your venison
For finer or fatter
Never ranged in a forest
Nor smoked on a platter.

Roast Venison 1

joint of venison, about 4lb (2kg)
olive oil
salt and pepper
1 tablespoon soy sauce
4 tablespoons honey
2 tablespoons lemon juice
1 clove of garlic, minced
pinch of cayenne pepper
salt and freshly ground black pepper
a little cornflour
½pt (300ml) cream
1 glass port wine

If the animal is fairly young it will not need larding or marinading. (My mother used to soak it all night in buttermilk and then rub it in butter instead of oil.) Massage as much olive oil into it as it will take, cover and roast in a fairly hot oven (375°F, 190°C, gas mark 5) till three parts cooked (allowing 20 minutes per pound). Take it out and dredge with salt and pepper. Next, mix together the soy sauce, honey, lemon juice, garlic, cayenne pepper, salt and freshly ground black pepper. Add sufficient olive oil to make a smooth paste and then paint the joint with it. Return the latter to the oven, but repeat the coats of 'paint' at intervals until it is all used up. Lift out the meat. Mix a little cornflour into the cream and add this, with the port wine, to the juices in the baking tin. Cook and stir over low heat until smooth, then pour over the venison and serve, accompanied by Cumberland sauce (page 176). *Serves 8.*

(If you are in a hurry, make a simple paste with a tablespoon of Dijon mustard mixed with 2 tablespoons of double cream.)

Roast Venison 2

joint of venison, interlarded
flour

The venison marinade

1 bottle red wine
½pt (300ml) olive oil
1 large onion, diced
1 clove garlic, minced
2 carrots, diced
2 sticks celery, diced
thyme, bay leaf
1 tablespoon mixed black and green peppercorns *or* juniper berries

For older roast venison, interlard and make a marinade. Mix the marinade ingredients together well. Put the venison in this and cover. Leave for at least twenty-four hours (forty-eight if possible), turning occasionally. Take out the venison, drain it well, roll in flour and fry in a deep casserole just enough to brown it. Strain the marinade, pour over, cover and roast in a fairly hot oven (375°F, 190°C, gas mark 5), allowing 20 minutes per pound. Serve with Cumberland sauce (page 176) or russet apples (allow 1 per person) baked with the venison for the last 25 minutes or so of the cooking time and then filled with cranberry jelly.

Down on the farm, ale is substituted for wine, and you could also use half wine and half water with 2 tablespoons of redcurrant jelly. For special occasions, use a whole bottle of port wine.

I might mention that Mario of the famous Caprice restaurant (and formerly for twenty-eight years at the equally well-known Ivy) always served venison slightly underdone and with a simple sauce comprising only the meat juices, enriched with brandy and cream.

See photograph facing page 144.

Venison Steaks

142

With young venison, it is possible to grill or fry steaks in the same way as beef steaks.

6 venison steaks
2oz (50g) butter
4oz (100g) salt pork, cubed
pinch of cayenne pepper
1 onion, minced
¼pt (150ml) stock
¼pt (150ml) red wine
¼pt (150ml) cream

Use a thick frying pan, put in the butter, cubed salt pork and cayenne pepper. Heat until the fat runs from the pork, fry the steaks till browned both sides and then remove them. Add to the pan the minced onion, stock and red wine. Cook gently for a few minutes till well mixed, then pour in the cream; put back the steaks to heat up. Serve with redcurrant jelly. *Serves 6.*

French Venison Pie

1½lb (¾kg) venison, cubed
½lb (225g) fat pork, diced
a few mushrooms, sliced
a little flour

For the marinade
See marinade for Roast Venison 2, page 141.

For the pastry
¾lb (350g) plain flour
4oz (100g) softened butter
2oz (50g) lard
2 egg yolks
1 egg for glaze

Our Continental friends are fond of venison pie, but they make their pastry in a rather different way to the shortcrust we use for our game pie. Make it this way:

Rub, with the fingertips, the softened butter and lard into the flour. Beat the egg yolks with ¼ pint (150ml) of cold water and mix with the flour and fat mixture, kneading it until it is a smooth, soft lump. Marinade the venison cubes as if for roasting. Both the pastry and venison are best left overnight. Next, fry the diced pork till the fat is extracted, add a few sliced mushrooms and sauté for a few minutes. Thicken with a little flour shaken in gradually, add the venison, with the marinade, and cook gently for about 1½ hours.

Roll out the pastry, butter a pie dish, put a funnel in the middle and a strip of pastry round the moistened rim of the dish. Put in the venison mixture, cover with a pastry lid, moistening and pressing the edges together to seal. Use any trimmings to decorate the pie. Brush over with beaten egg and bake in a moderate oven (350°F, 180°C, gas mark 4) for about 35 minutes. *Serves 6.*

Venison Casserole

2lb (1kg) venison
dripping for frying
2 onions, chopped
2 carrots, chopped
2 bacon rashers, chopped
1 tablespoon flour
1½ pints (¾ litre) stock
1 glass Madeira
1 teaspoon brown sugar
pinch of allspice
salt and black pepper
bouquet garni
2–3 tablespoons redcurrant jelly

For the potato dumplings

1lb (450g) potatoes, grated
5 slices white bread
1 tablespoon minced parsley
salt and pepper
1 small onion, minced
1 egg, beaten
a little flour

Brown the venison all over in dripping, take it from the pan and put aside. Fry the onions, carrots and rashers of bacon for a few minutes and remove these also. Add the flour to the stock, and stir until smooth. Add the Madeira wine, brown sugar, allspice, salt, black pepper and a *bouquet garni*. Put the venison in a deep casserole with the sautéd vegetables and bacon, pour the liquid over and cook in a moderate oven (350°F, 180°C, gas mark 4) for 2½–3 hours. Put in 2–3 tablespoons of redcurrant jelly, stir till melted. Serve with potato dumplings, which are made as follows:

Wash, peel and grate the potatoes. Soak the slices of bread in cold water, squeeze hard till almost dry, then mash with the minced parsley, salt and pepper, minced onion, potatoes and a well-beaten egg. Form into balls, roll in flour, drop into boiling water and cook gently for 10 minutes. *Serves 6.*

A South African friend tells me that the *duiker* is considered very good, and also the springbok, although the latter is rare in the Western Province. But the steenbok and grysbok are very plentiful in some districts and are very good to eat. The cooking seems to be very similar to our own, the meat being larded, marinaded and roasted.

There is an old saying about 'making a person eat humble pie'. Somehow, this has for long been considered to mean that the said person has been brought low and made to apologize. I have only recently learned that, way back in the seventeenth century, deer's offals (heart, liver, etc.) were called 'umbles' and were, in fact, given to the head huntsman, who had them made into a sort of glorified giblet pie, which he shared with his fellow workers.

Venison à Franche

144 joint of venison
olive oil
wine
black pepper
1 onion, finely chopped
1 carrot, finely chopped
1 stick of celery, finely chopped
1 tablespoon flour
a few mushrooms
1 tablespoon tomato purée
pinch of mixed herbs
½pt (300ml) stock
2 glasses red wine

In this French method the venison tenderloin is cut into round steaks or escallops. Lay these in a shallow dish and cover with a mixture of olive oil, wine and black pepper. Leave for two hours.

In another 3 tablespoons of olive oil gently fry the finely chopped onion, carrot and celery until soft. Stir the flour in slowly and when brown add the mushrooms, tomato purée, mixed herbs, stock and red wine. Bring to the boil, pour over the venison and bake for 45 minutes in a moderate oven (350°F, 180°C, gas mark 4). *Serves 6.*

Haunch of venison, marinading in wine
and aromatics
See page 141 for recipe

12

Hare and Rabbit

The receipts of cookery are swelled to
a volume,
but a good stomach excels them all.
William Penn

Pytchley Game Pie
See page 167 for recipe

146 Probably all of us have, at some time, heard someone say, 'as mad as a March hare', and vaguely wondered why mad and why March. A long time ago, an author or poet used the phrase 'marsh hare' and a controversy ensued as to whether March or marsh was correct. Both hares and rabbits were associated with fertility rites and considered sacred to the goddess Eastre, the forerunner of our Easter. However, March is the mating season for hares, when the males, like many other animals, birds and even insects display their charms in gloss of fur, splendour of feather, or elegance designed to appeal to the opposite sex. In the case of hares, they apparently annually indulge in such spectacular undulating convulsions that to humans they appear quite mad. They throw caution to the wind and appear in great numbers. Cobbett, in his *Rural Rides,* talks of seeing an acre of hares. Of course, *Homo sapiens* doesn't have any periodic seasons, having a built-in perpetual urge to surge and merge. There was once an old belief that hares change their sex annually, and in an enthralling book, *The Leaping Hare* (Faber), a possible explanation is given: 'It was said that the female hare escaped from the ark and was drowned, leaving only one. So God gave him the power to bear children.'

Scientists have decided that hares (the mountain or blue hares) have probably been in Britain since the closing phase of the Ice Age, but the brown hare was originally brought over from Iceland by sportsmen.

There are many superstitions regarding hares. Ben Jonson proclaimed that 'a witch is a kind of hare,' but Samuel Pepys carried around a hare's foot for luck. He wrote, 'I never had a fit of the colic since I wore it.'

Another superstition claimed that a hare passing in front of you brought good luck, but if it ran behind you it was an ill omen; and I think it was Shakespeare (in *Henry IV*) who implied its flesh generated melancholy.

In law, hares are game and it is illegal for them to be sold in shops between 1 March and 31 July. Still, if you have acquired a hare, make the best and the most of it. First determine its age by tearing its ear. If that can be done easily, it is young. If it's a tough ear, it's a tough creature. Look also at its claws which, sharp when young, become blunt with age. Young or old, it should be hung, without opening, for some days and then paunched, just before skinning, cleaning and cooking. Generally speaking, young hares are best roasted and the older ones jugged, stewed or cooked in a casserole.

Skinning, paunching and trussing

Whenever a hare is mentioned in connection with cooking, jugged hares automatically come to mind. I think the word jugged probably derives from the tall brown earthenware jars in which food was cooked (I still have the one my grandmother used). I have already mentioned my own first calamitous effort to jug a hare, but since then I have become older and, I hope, wiser. At least, I've been shown by an expert how it should be done, and the first thing is to persuade someone to skin and paunch it for you, saving every drop of blood in a separate vessel.

First, cut off the feet with a sharp knife. Then slit the skin along the belly and ease it away from the flesh gradually. Pull the skin over the hind legs, then up towards the head and finally off the forelegs and head.

Proceed with paunching the hare or rabbit by first cutting open the belly with a scissors. Remove all the internal organs. Retain the kidneys, liver and heart for use in a sauce. Take care not to break the gall bladder. Keep any blood (a few drops of vinegar added will prevent it coagulating). This can be used later to thicken the gravy or sauce. Finally, wipe out the insides with a clean, damp cloth.

If you intend to roast the animal whole, sever the sinews of the hind legs at the thighs so that they can be brought forward, and tie them close to the body with skewers (or a trussing needle) and string. Tie the forelegs in the same way.

Rabbit skins

With so many synthetic furs now available, it is doubtful if anyone would bother to cure the skins of rabbits or any other fur-coated creature. However, it costs little but time and patience. Stretch the skins, fur side downwards and secure firmly on a board. Scrape off all the surplus flesh or fat. Pour 1 quart (1 litre) of boiling water over 1lb (450g) of alum. Let it cool, add ½ pint (300ml) of cold water and a heaped tablespoon of sodium bicarbonate. Sponge the skin twice daily for about a week, then smear with oil or fat (adding more if necessary) and work this in till the skin is soft and supple.

Jugged Hare

1 hare
blood of the hare
1 onion, chopped
2 carrots
few sticks of celery
olive oil for frying
a little flour
1½ pints (900ml) meat stock
1 tablespoon redcurrant jelly
salt and pepper
4 tablespoons port wine
12 triangles stale white bread, fried in butter
    until golden and drained on absorbent
    paper

For the marinade

1 onion, chopped
2 whole cloves of garlic
2 bay leaves
4 tablespoons olive oil
4 tablespoons white wine vinegar
salt and pepper

For the forcemeat

the heart, liver and kidneys of the hare,
    minced
their weight in minced bacon
1 onion, chopped
1 cup breadcrumbs
2 teaspoons mixed herbs
salt and pepper
1 egg, beaten

Cut up the hare into serving pieces and put into a basin. Mix the marinade ingredients together and cover the hare with this. Move it around from time to time, but let it have at least 6 hours soaking.

Meanwhile, fry the chopped onion, carrots, and celery in olive oil and put in a stew jar (retaining the oil in the pan).

Take the meat and the garlic from the marinade, dry and flour the pieces and fry in the oil to brown, put with the vegetables and the marinade in the stew jar, add the boiling meat stock, redcurrant jelly, salt and pepper and cook in a slow oven (300°F, 150°C, gas mark 2) for 2 hours. Finally, put in the bloody gore and the port wine; simmer gently for a few minutes.

While the hare is cooking, make some forcemeat balls by finely mincing the heart, kidneys and liver, the minced bacon, chopped onion, breadcrumbs, mixed herbs, salt and pepper. Bind with a beaten egg. Roll in flour, put into a pan with a pint of stock, cover and simmer gently for half an hour before serving with the hare. Arrange the croûtes around the edge of the dish.

Glazed small onions and red cabbage make a nice accompaniment to this dish. Plainly cooked rice or a purée of potato would also be very good. *Serves 6.*

Roasted Hare

1 hare, jointed
3 tablespoons cream

For the marinade
½pt (300ml) red wine
4 tablespoons olive oil
a few bay leaves
salt and pepper

For the forcemeat
ingredients as in preceding recipe for
    jugged hare.

Put the prepared hare in a deep vessel. Mix
the marinade ingredients together and cover
it with this. Leave for a few hours and turn
occasionally. Make forcemeat, as for the
jugged hare above, and put this, without
cooking, into the cavity, drawing the edges
together and pinning with small skewers (or
sew loosely with needle and thread). Cover
and cook in a moderate oven (350°F, 180°C,
gas mark 4) for 2 hours, basting occasionally.
Remove the hare and the bay leaves, stir the
cream into the juice and serve separately.
Serves 6.

Lièvre Hongroise

1 hare, jointed
seasoned flour
butter
½pt (300ml) white sauce (see page 172)
    or cream

For the marinade
1 glass white wine
1 glass water
a few cloves
3–4 crushed green peppercorns

Cut the prepared hare into joints, put it in
the marinade and leave overnight if possible.
Then remove the pieces, dry, roll in seasoned
flour, and sauté in butter till well browned.
Put into a baking dish, heat the marinade,
the white sauce or cream, pour over the hare
and bake in a slow oven (300°F, 150°C, gas
mark 2) for 45 minutes. If liked, fried onions,
mushrooms or tomatoes can be added before
cooking. *Serves 6.*

Hare Pudding

Among my souvenirs, I have a recipe from *The Art of Cookery Made Plain and Easy* by Hannah Glasse (1747). I know not whence it came, nor can I trace anything about Hannah, but here are the instructions:

Take your hare when it is cased [presumably, skinned and paunched] and make a pudding. With the head and neck, the liver, heart and kidneys, some salt and black pepper, cook to a good gravy. Make a crust with a pound and a half of flour and two spoons of raising powder, three parts of a pound of suet chopped fine and water to mix. Roll out, keep a large round part to cover the top of a large basin which should have butter rubbed over it inside and then lined with the pastry. Put in the hare, cut into pieces to fit, pour in the strained gravy, cover with the pastry round, tie on a pudding cloth and boil for two hours.

Lièvre Suisse

An American friend, visiting her son who held a diplomatic appointment in Switzerland, was enthusiastic about the hare served at a dinner she attended. I gather it was prepared as for jugged hare but $\frac{1}{4}$ pint (150ml) vinegar was added to the blood and kept very cold. The hare was cut into serving pieces, covered with chopped onions, carrots, parsley, salt and pepper and then enough red wine poured over to completely cover. It was left overnight, then the meat taken out and fried with pieces of fat pork in butter till brown. The marinade was strained and put, with the hare and pork, in a casserole and cooked in a slow oven (300°F, 150°C, gas mark 2) for $2\frac{1}{2}$ hours. Finally the blood was added and simmered (but not boiled) for a few minutes before serving.

Saddle of Hare with Chestnuts

saddle and hindquarters of a young hare
3 thin slices of pork fat
$\frac{1}{2}$lb (225g) chestnuts, weighed when baked and peeled
The marinade from Lièvre Hongroise on previous page

For the sauce

2 floz (50ml) brandy
2 tablespoons cream
6 tablespoons chicken velouté (page 173)
1 tablespoon french mustard

Marinate the hare for 4–6 hours or overnight, then strain the marinade into a bowl and set aside. Dry the hare well, tie on the slices of pork fat, and brown it in a hot oven (425°F, 210°C, gas mark 7), turning it often. Heat the marinade liquid, add it to the roasting tin and continue cooking the hare, basting it from time to time, allowing 15 minutes per pound. When the hare is cooked, remove it from the oven and keep hot.

To make the sauce, deglaze the roasting tin with the brandy, add the cream and reduce it a little by boiling it. Then thicken with the velouté sauce and mustard. Reheat over a moderate heat, and check the seasoning.

Cut the saddle into 4 pieces and serve on a heated dish, garnished with the chestnuts, and strain over the sauce. *Serves 4.*

Rabbit

I know a cat, who makes a habit
Of eating nothing else but rabbit,
And when he's finished, licks his paws
So's not to waste the onion sauce.

T. S. Eliot, *Old Possum's Book of Practical Cats*

Rabbits are not classified as game, but if you 'trespass in search' of them, you commit an offence against the game laws.

I mentioned earlier that, living on a farm far from any shops and long before benefit of refrigerators, emergency rations often meant rabbits. My father would take his gun, go down to the woods where there was a rabbit warren and come back with a bunny, or sometimes two. And I still remember vividly begging him to take me with him – I was only four to five years old – and he let me go on condition that I remained silent. I wasn't accustomed to being silent (I never have been!) but I promised. He was over six feet tall and led me along, then paused and whispered, 'Keep still'. I stood as stationary as Lot's wife, when above me there was the sudden sound of an explosion and I was so taken by surprise, that I sat down more suddenly than I've ever since been seated.

And so rabbit was almost a regular contribution to our larder but, for variety, we had them roasted or stewed, in puddings and pies and with different seasonings, flavourings and accompaniments, many of the dishes being similar to those made with hare. In his *Diary of a Country Parson*, Woodforde writes of rabbit as 'a good ordinary dinner'.

Unlike hares, however, rabbits are paunched immediately after killing and before being hung. Fred Taylor carries out that operation before leaving the fields. I wish chefs wouldn't use the word 'paunch' for de-gutting hares and rabbits. Compared with some members of *Homo sapiens* they don't have paunches (but they do retain their own teeth and sex appeal right into old age!).

With the waning of myxomatosis it seems that we shall once more be plagued with rabbits – a pest to farmers, although they do provide food for predators like foxes, stoats and weasels, which in their absence made inroads into the game populations. Shooting them may become fashionable sport and wild rabbits are, or seem to be, far more tasty than those bred for the table or the frozen ones from Australia or China. Perhaps it is because their diet includes so varied an assortment of fresh vegetation and herbs.

An American author has said, 'There's about as many ways of cooking rabbit, as there is of courting a gal,' but, generally speaking, young rabbits are best roasted, braised or baked, and older ones used in stews, casseroles, puddings and pies.

Roast Rabbit

1 rabbit, jointed
½pt (300ml) stock, or water

For the marinade
vinegar
water

For the stuffing
2–3 large onions
4oz (100g) breadcrumbs
1 tablespoon minced sage
salt and pepper
a little softened butter

You can marinade rabbit in the same way and stuff with the same forcemeat as used in jugged hare (see page 148), but in our family (where the farmer's wife was responsible for dairy, poultry and kitchen garden), time for cooking was limited and a rabbit, dutifully skinned and cleaned by my father, was put in a marinade of half vinegar and half water while an onion stuffing was prepared. This was made by boiling the whole onions till soft, chopping them, adding the breadcrumbs, minced sage, salt and pepper and binding it with a little softened butter. This was then put into the rabbit which was sewn together (rather crudely), put into a baking dish with the stock or water, covered and cooked in a slow oven (200°F, 100°C, gas mark 1) for 1½ hours, with an occasional basting. *Serves 4.*

An alternative stuffing was sometimes made by mixing 2 tablespoons of chopped suet with 3 tablespoons of breadcrumbs, a dessertspoon of chopped parsley, the grated rind and juice of a lemon, salt and pepper, and binding it with a beaten egg. If breadcrumbs aren't readily available and time is of the essence, soak a thick slice of bread in water, squeeze out the liquid and use this as breadcrumbs. Serve with a sauce made from a tin of mushroom soup heated with a tablespoon of mushroom ketchup.

German Stewed Rabbit

This is sometimes called *Hasenpfeffer*.

1 rabbit
seasoned flour
½lb (225g) fat pork, diced
1 tablespoon butter
the rabbit's heart, liver and kidneys
or 4oz (100g) calf's liver
1 large onion, chopped
1 clove garlic, crushed
6 peppercorns
1 tablespoon flour
pinch of oregano and marjoram
salt and pepper
grated peel of 1 lemon
2 glasses red wine
½pt (300ml) stock

For the marinade

vinegar
water

Marinade the rabbit for twenty-four hours in half vinegar and half water. Dry well, cut into medium-sized portions and roll in seasoned flour. In a large casserole, fry the diced fat pork, add the butter, then the rabbit. Sauté, turning the pieces until well browned. Mince and add the rabbit's heart, liver and kidneys with the chopped onion, crushed clove of garlic and peppercorns. Sprinkle over the flour, add the oregano and marjoram, salt, pepper, grated lemon peel, one glass of red wine and the stock. Simmer gently for an hour, then add the second glass of red wine and cook for another 30 minutes. Serve with small frankfurter sausages and boiled and buttered noodles. *Serves 4.*

Spanish Stewed Rabbit

1 rabbit, jointed
flour, seasoned with garlic salt and
    black pepper
oil for frying
1 large onion, chopped
1 green pepper, diced
1 small can pimentos
2–3 potatoes
1 large can of peas

For the marinade

1 cup of vinegar
½ cup of wine
1 large onion, chopped
2 bay leaves

This recipe actually came to me from America, but it is said to be of Spanish origin.

Combine the vinegar, wine, chopped onion, bay leaves and enough water to cover the jointed rabbit. Leave to marinade overnight, then remove the meat, dry it and roll in the seasoned flour. Fry in hot fat till browned all over, then remove and cook the chopped onion and diced green pepper in the remaining fat till tender. Put the rabbit, the marinade and the onion and pepper into a casserole with a small can of pimentos and cook gently for 2 hours. Add 2 or 3 potatoes and a large can of peas. Cook again till these vegetables are tender. *Serves 4.*

Hunters Pie

1 rabbit
12 peppercorns
a little butter
4 bacon rashers
4 hard-boiled eggs
salt and pepper
a little meat extract

For the shortcrust pastry

10 oz (275g) self-raising flour
6oz (175g) cooking fat
cold water to mix
1 beaten egg to glaze

Cook the rabbit in slightly salted water or stock with the peppercorns. Make a shortcrust pastry with the self-raising flour, cooking fat and sufficient cold water to mix. Butter a pie dish and put a wide strip of pastry around the moistened rim and about 2 inches (5cm) inside. Cut the rabbit into small joints and pack in with the chopped bacon and hard-boiled eggs distributed between the pieces. Season with salt and pepper. Dissolve a little meat extract into the stock and pour over the rabbit. Place a pie funnel in the centre. Moisten the bands of pastry round the pie dish, lay over the pastry cover, pressing the edges together to seal. Trim neatly and use the leftover strips to form leaves for decoration around the centre. To enhance the appearance, brush the top with beaten egg. Put in a hot oven (425°F, 210°C, gas mark 7) for 15 minutes, then lower to moderate (350°F, 180°C, gas mark 4) and cook for an hour. *Serves 4.*

You can use sausage meat with a sage seasoning instead of the eggs and bacon.

Rabbit Galantine

1 young rabbit
sausage meat
forcemeat (as for Baked Pike, page 65)
3–4 hard-boiled eggs
aspic

This needs a little patience, but the result makes it worthwhile. You need a fairly young rabbit. First, remove the head, cut right down the front and take out the bones, keeping the flesh in one piece. Lay it flat on its back, cover with greaseproof paper and roll it gently, like pastry. Then remove the paper and spread with sausage meat, then a layer of seasoned forcemeat. Roll it up carefully, putting a row of hard-boiled eggs along the middle. Secure with a few tiny skewers, cover with greaseproof paper, put in a pudding cloth, secure with string, put into boiling water and simmer for 2 hours. Take out, unwrap and, as it cools, spoon over a little aspic glaze occasionally. Serve cold with a green salad. *Serves 4–6.*

For rabbits young and rabbits old
For rabbits hot and rabbits cold
For rabbits tender, rabbits tough
We thank the Lord, but we've had enough.

Farmhouse Rabbit

1 young rabbit, jointed
1 onion, sliced
generous pinch of mace
1pt (600ml) milk
1 tablespoon flour
a little milk
salt and pepper
a knob of butter
freshly chopped parsley

Put the jointed rabbit in a pan with the sliced onion, mace and milk. Simmer gently, stirring occasionally, for an hour, then thicken with the flour mixed with a little cold milk, season with salt and pepper, finish with a knob of butter and garnish with chopped parsley. *Serves 4.*

Rabbit Pudding

This can be made like Hannah Glasse's hare pudding (see page 150), and I think a few mushrooms enhance the flavour.

Postscript

Before we say farewell to rabbits, you may like to know what Mrs Clarence Church, of Cahhoun (Kentucky), has to say about cooking them:

I most usually soak 'em in salt water a few hours, then roll in flour and fry slow, place in roaster, cover with water and a lid and bake 2 to 3 hours, when meat is falling from bone. You have a thin gravy there; that's wonderful on hot biscuit and mashed potatoes.

I cook squirrel this way – I have also cooked coon the same way, cutting it up in pieces.

Then I've cut the meat raw from rabbits and ground it and mixed with pork sausage meat and fried it and everyone liked that real well. More sage and seasoning can be added (I only added pepper and salt).

I've also ground up cooked rabbit, added boiled eggs, pickles and salad dressing and made sandwiches out of that. And ground up raw rabbit meat and mixed it with eggs, butter, oatmeal, tomato juice, salt and pepper and baked as a meat loaf.

Then I boiled the bones, picked off the meat, spread that in an 8-inch square pan. Take 2 cups of the broth, mix up 2 heaped tablespoonsful of flour in cold water, cook as a cream sauce, pour over the meat, top with baking powder biscuit and bake.

A good rabbit cook can think up nigh as many ways to cook a rabbit as there's rabbits to cook.

Squirrel

Recently, I read an article about squirrels by our intrepid friend Fred J. Taylor, author and angler, camp organizer, chef *par excellence* and a frequent visitor to his numerous friends in America. He wrote about the way the British people reacted with abhorrence to the very idea of eating squirrels, yet the grey squirrels are a menace and, in fact, even a worse pest than rabbits. They are considered delicacies among our cousins in the USA, who will tell you that young fried squirrel is the tastiest meat there is. They are prepared like young rabbits and this is one of their favourite ways of cooking them:

Brunswick Stew

1 squirrel
seasoned flour
fat for frying
4oz (100g) fat pork
3 large onions, sliced
1 clove garlic, crushed
3 tomatoes, peeled and chopped
3 red peppers, seeded and thinly sliced
3 cups water
2 cups dry cider
pinch of thyme
1 tablespoon chopped parsley
1 teaspoon Worcestershire sauce
salt and pepper
3 tablespoons flour

Soak the squirrel in salted water or vinegar and water for at least twenty-four hours. Dry, dip in seasoned flour and fry in hot fat until browned all over. Then put the squirrel into a casserole. Fry the fat pork with the onions and garlic for a few minutes. Add to the squirrel with the tomatoes and red peppers, water, dry cider or vinegar, thyme, chopped parsley, Worcestershire sauce and salt and pepper. Cover and cook in a moderate oven (350°F, 180°C, gas mark 4) for an hour. Mix the 3 tablespoons of flour with water and stir into the sauce in the pot. Reheat slowly for about 15 minutes and serve with lima beans. *Serves 2.*

In passing, the fat pork is usually pig's cheek and is called 'hog's jowl'.

Way down in Tennessee, the tomatoes and red peppers are replaced by soaked and pipped prunes.

In Indiana, they cook the squirrels with sauerkraut; in Missouri, with dumplings; in Detroit with celery, mushrooms and cream. But as Mrs Church of Kentucky (the ingenious rabbit manipulator) might say, 'Nobody swipes a recipe, less'n he likes it.' Here's one I swiped from a Missouri magazine:

Bumper Bushytail

2 squirrels
tarragon vinegar
1 onion, diced
1 stick of celery, diced
1 carrot, diced
salt
1 bay leaf
heaped teaspoon curry powder
2 medium potatoes, sliced
bunch of parsley
mushrooms (optional)

Prepare as in the previous recipe, then put the squirrels in a monster pot and cover with water laced with tarragon vinegar. Simmer for 2 hours, then put in the diced onion, celery and carrot. Add salt, the bay leaf and curry powder. Cook 2 more hours, when the meat should be dropping off the bones and the said bones can be fished out. Next drop in the sliced potatoes, and the bunch of parsley. If a cupful of mushrooms is handy, toss them in too. Simmer for another half an hour and then eat hearty. *Serves 3–4.*

13
Game Miscellanea

Your supper is like the Hidalgo's dinner,
Very little meat and a great deal of tablecloth.

The Spanish Student

Introduction

160   The ways in which left-over game can be used are almost endless, and an ingenious cook can produce a vast variety of dishes. Minced game can, of course, be used with the other usual ingredients to make stuffing for new and younger birds, or as a filling for omelettes, pancakes, meat loaf and rissoles, or as a stuffing for marrows and other vegetables.

Game with Potatoes

This Swedish dish, made with potatoes and cold meat, is very suitable for cold game.

several cooked, whole potatoes
2oz (50g) butter
3oz (75g) diced bacon
1 onion, minced
about 8oz (225g) cooked, cold game, sliced
salt and pepper
chopped parsley
Worcestershire sauce
1 fried egg per person (optional)

The sliced, cooked potatoes are sautéd in butter, drained and kept warm. In the remaining butter, the diced bacon is fried with the minced onion and cooked till soft, then the cold meat is added and the whole seasoned with salt and pepper. Next the potatoes are returned to the pan, with chopped parsley and a little sauce (such as Worcestershire sauce). The mixture is then put in a hot dish and served, sometimes topped with a fried egg for each diner. *Serves 2–3.*

Viande à l'Hiver

This French dish, originally made with cold meat, is also adaptable for cold game.

12oz (350g) cooked cold game, diced
2 onions, minced
1 clove garlic, crushed
olive oil
1 tablespoon Dijon mustard
1 tablespoon wine vinegar
1 tablespoon flour
½pt (300ml) stock
1 tablespoon soft brown sugar
6 drops Tabasco sauce
salt and pepper
1oz fried crumbs
butter

Cook the minced onions and crushed clove of garlic in olive oil until soft. Add the Dijon mustard, wine vinegar and flour. Stir well, gradually add the stock. When smooth, stir in the soft brown sugar, Tabasco sauce, salt and pepper.

Put the diced meat or game in a greased fireproof dish, pour over the sauce, sprinkle with browned breadcrumbs and dot with butter. Bake in a fairly hot oven (375°F, 190°C, gas mark 5) for about 20 minutes. Serve with boiled rice. *Serves 4.*

Game Casserole

4oz (100g) white breadcrumbs
butter
about ½lb (225g) sliced mushrooms
1lb (450g) cold, cooked game, diced
mixed herbs
salt and pepper
½pt (300ml) chicken stock
¼pt (150ml) thick cream

Fry the white breadcrumbs in butter and put half of them in a buttered casserole. Sauté the sliced mushrooms for a few minutes and mix with the diced cold game, mixed herbs, salt and pepper. Heat the chicken stock, add the thick cream and pour over the game. Top with the rest of the breadcrumbs and bake in a pre-heated oven (375°F, 190°C, gas mark 5) for about 20 minutes. The two foregoing recipes can both be prepared beforehand. *Serves 6.*

Hash Supreme

American friends told me this simple way of using cold game.

1lb (450g) cold, cooked game, diced
⅛pt (75ml) cream
1pt (600ml) *béchamel* sauce (see page 172)
½pt (300ml) milk
2 tablespoons butter
2 tablespoons flour
1 onion, grated
pinch of salt
3 tablespoons grated Parmesan cheese
3 egg yolks

For this hash, dice the cold game meat and heat with the cream for 10 minutes, then add to the hot *béchamel* sauce and put in a shallow baking dish.

Scald the milk (do not boil) in a saucepan. In another pan, melt the butter, stir in the flour, add the grated onion, salt, Parmesan cheese and finally the scalded milk. Cook over low heat for about 5 minutes and set aside to cool. Beat the egg yolks, add to the *béchamel* hash gradually and finally top with the cheese sauce and grill till golden brown. *Serves 6.*

Patti Casserole

1pt (600ml) *béchamel* sauce (see page 172)
½lb (225g) pasta pieces
1lb (450g) cold, cooked game, diced
¼lb (100g) cooked ham, diced
½lb (225g) mushrooms, sliced
1oz (25g) butter
1 glass dry white wine or sherry
2 egg yolks
½pt (300ml) thick cream
salt and pepper
nutmeg

First, make the *béchamel* sauce. Meanwhile cook the pasta pieces in boiling water. Dice the cold cooked game and ham and sauté the mushrooms in a little butter. Add the glass of dry white wine or sherry.

Beat the 2 egg yolks, stir in the thick cream. Add to the *béchamel* sauce, stir well, put in the game and ham, season well with salt and pepper and nutmeg and finally add the mushrooms.

Butter a casserole, put in the pasta, then the game mixture and bake in a hot oven (400°F, 200°C, gas mark 6) for 20–25 minutes. *Serves 6.*

As an alternative, use aubergines instead of mushrooms.

Pelotas

1lb (450g) diced cold game
2 tomatoes, peeled, seeded and chopped
1 onion, chopped
1 teaspoon mixed herbs
salt and freshly ground black pepper
stock
a few olives, stoned
a few green peppercorns, crushed
1 tablespoon seedless raisins
3–4 slices of bread
a little milk
2 eggs
1oz (25g) breadcrumbs
1oz (25g) butter

Fry the peeled and seeded tomatoes with the chopped onion. Add the mixed herbs, salt and black pepper. When soft add the diced cold game and enough stock to moisten. Add the olives, green peppercorns and raisins. Put in a buttered casserole. Soak the slices of bread in milk, drain and cover the mixture. Beat the eggs, add salt and pepper and pour over the top. Finally, sprinkle with breadcrumbs, dot with butter and bake in a fairly hot oven (375°F, 190°C, gas mark 5) for about 25 minutes or until the top is crisp and brown. *Serves 6.*

Game Soufflé

1 tablespoon butter
1 tablespoon flour
1pt (600ml) scalded milk
2oz (50g) white breadcrumbs
1lb (450g) minced game
1 tablespoon minced parsley
1 teaspoon salt
pinch of cayenne pepper
2 eggs, separated
a little butter

This is a super concoction. Melt the butter in a saucepan over a low heat, mix in the flour, slowly add the scalded milk, stirring smoothly. Bring to the boil and add the white breadcrumbs. After a few minutes, remove from the heat and stir in the minced game, minced parsley, salt, cayenne pepper and the yolks of the 2 eggs, well beaten.

Whip the egg whites till stiff and fold into the mixture. Put in buttered two-pint (1 litre) soufflé dish, bake in a hot oven (425°F, 220°C, gas mark 7) for about 20 minutes and serve *instanter*. *Serves 6.*

Game Pies and Puddings

For many of us, game pie is the archetypal sportsman's dish. It is hearty enough to satisfy the hungriest, and handsome enough to give *anyone* an appetite. As well as this, it is infinitely adaptable and guaranteed to make the most of whatever game you may have.

Most of the recipes in this section require a pastry lid. The recipe below will be suitable for any of these.

Savoury shortcrust pastry

8oz (225g) plain flour
2oz (50g) butter
2oz (50g) lard
pinch of salt
a little cold water

Put the flour into a large mixing bowl with the butter and lard, cut into pieces, and the salt. Rub the flour and fat lightly between the fingertips until the mixture resembles fine crumbs. Mix to a stiffish paste with a little cold water.

To cover a Game Pie

First roll out the pastry to about 1 inch (2½cm) larger than the top of the pie dish. Then cut a rim of pastry about ½ inch (1cm) wide to fit the rim of the dish. Moisten the rim of the dish and press on the pastry strip. Moisten this and place the lid on. Press down well to seal the edges and trim off the excess pastry. If you wish, re-roll the pastry trimmings and cut leaves to decorate the pie. Dampen these also and arrange in place. Finally, glaze with beaten egg.

Family
Rolypoly (Boiled)

1 large onion, minced
2 rashers bacon, chopped
a little fat
1 tablespoon flour
¼pt (150ml) stock
½lb (225g) cooked, cold game, diced
salt and freshly ground black pepper
pinch of cayenne pepper

For the suet crust

4oz (100g) suet
½lb (225g) plain flour
pinch of baking powder
pinch of salt
a little cold water

Sauté the minced onion with the chopped
bacon in a little added fat. Stir the flour into
the stock and add the diced game, salt, black
pepper and a pinch of cayenne pepper. (A
cold, diced potato can be added to stretch
the mixture if necessary.)

Make a suet crust with the suet, baking
powder, flour and salt, mixing to a stiff paste
with cold water. Roll out, spread the mixture
over, moisten the edges, roll up, put into a
floured pudding cloth, drop in boiling water
and simmer for 1½ hours. *Serves 4.*

Baked Rolypoly

pie ingredients as opposite
shortcrust pastry (see page 164)

Make the shortcrust pastry with the flour,
lard and butter, salt and enough water to
make a stiff paste. Roll out, spread the mixture
over, moisten the edges, roll up, sealing the
join, which should be at the bottom. Bake in
a moderate oven (350°F, 180°C, gas mark 4)
for half an hour. *Serves 4.*

Oregon Tart

2 cups cooked game, chopped
½ cup raw carrot, shredded
2 tablespoons minced onion
1 teaspoon dry mustard
1 tablespoon grated horseradish
pinch of mixed herbs
salt and pepper
1 egg, beaten
shortcrust pastry (see page 164 – but make
    double the quantity)

Mix the chopped, cooked game with the
carrots, minced onion, dry mustard and grated
horseradish. Add the mixed herbs, salt and
pepper. Moisten with the beaten egg mixed
with a little stock. Roll out one-third of the
pastry and line a pie dish with it; spread the
mixture over, leaving a ½in. margin clear.
Dampen this. Roll out the remaining pastry,
cover the pie, pinching the edges all round
to seal. Make a steam-hole in the centre and
bake the tart for 40–45 minutes in a moderate
oven (350°F, 180°C, gas mark 4). *Serves 6.*

Fred Taylor's Game Pie (hot)

Game pie is one of the great traditional British dishes and the majority of general cookery books include a recipe. However, there are variations, depending perhaps on family favourites or different regional areas. The one which I still recall with pleasure was made at my home by my versatile friend, Fred Taylor, and he has been kind enough to give me his recipe and also instructions for one to eat cold.

1lb (450g) game
seasoned flour
a little fat
2 onions, diced
2 carrots, diced
4oz (100g) mushrooms, diced
game stock
salt and pepper
shortcrust pastry
1 egg, beaten with 1 teaspoon water

1 Trim meat from the game and cut into dice. Pressure-cook remaining carcases until meat falls off and a concentrated stock remains.

2 Toss the meat dice in seasoned flour and brown in hot shallow fat. Brown the diced onions, carrots and mushrooms in same fat. Cover all with stock and cook slowly until the meat is tender and the liquid thick. Season to taste.

3 Place in a large pie dish. Place a pie funnel in the centre to support the pastry top, cover with shortcrust pastry made from pure lard, brush with diluted beaten egg and bake in a fairly hot oven (400°F, 200°C, gas mark 6) for about 45 minutes. *Serves 4.*

Fred Taylor's Game Pie (cold)

1lb (450g) game
$\frac{1}{4}$lb (100g) not too lean pork
$\frac{1}{4}$lb (100g) wholemeal breadcrumbs
a little milk
salt and pepper
sage
1 egg yolk, beaten with 1 teaspoon cold water
1oz (25g) gelatine

1 Repeat stage 1 of the previous recipe (cutting dice *extra* small).

2 Add the pork and wholemeal breadcrumbs (soaked in a little milk and squeezed) to the game. Add liberal salt, pepper and sage seasoning.

3 Pack all into a pie crust paste (hot-water paste for raised pies, ordinary shortcrust pastry, see page 164, for tinned pies). Bake for 15 minutes or so at 450°F, 230°C, gas mark 8. Glaze with beaten egg and then lower temperature to 350°F, 180°C, gas mark 4 and cook for a further $1\frac{1}{2}$ hours. Add the gelatine to 1 pint (600ml) of the reduced stock and, when the pie has cooled, pour this through the steam-escape hole in the pastry and allow to set. *Serves 6.*

Welsh Game Pie

On a journey across Wales some years ago, this game pie appeared on the menu of the hotel where I stayed. I was given the recipe:

equal quantities of cooked game and
   minced beef
a little butter
salt and black pepper
chopped leeks
stock
shortcrust pastry (see recipe page 164)
1 egg yolk mixed with a little milk

Butter a large pie dish. Mix an equal quantity of cooked game and minced beef, season with salt and black pepper. Put a layer of meat in the dish, cover with chopped leeks, then continue with alternate layers, finishing with leeks. Pour in stock almost to the top. Place a pie funnel in the centre to support the pastry top. Cover with the shortcrust pastry. Brush with beaten egg and a little milk, bake in a moderate oven (350°F, 180°C, gas mark 4) and cook for 1–1½ hours.

Devonshire Game Pie

Mince cold game, add half the quantity of cooked ham and one or two apples and a large onion, peeled and sliced. Season with sage, salt and pepper. Add stock and place a pie funnel in the centre to support the pastry top. Cover with the pastry and cook in a moderate oven (350°F, 180°C, gas mark 4) for 1–1½ hours.

Pytchley Game Pie

2–3 game birds (e.g. pheasant)
2 carrots, sliced
few sticks of celery, sliced
2 onions, sliced
thyme, parsley, bay leaf
a little meat extract
4oz (100g) fat bacon
4oz (100g) calf's liver
game giblets, diced
4oz (100g) chopped mushrooms
salt and pepper
shortcrust pastry (see recipe page 164)

Remove the flesh from the birds, and cook the bones and giblets with the carrots, celery, onions and herbs until all the goodness is extracted. Put aside till cold and remove any fat, strain and colour with a little meat extract. Fry the game pieces with diced fat bacon and calf's liver, the giblets, chopped mushrooms and seasoning.

Fill a buttered pie dish, add the game stock and place a pie funnel in the centre to support the pastry crust. Cover with the shortcrust pastry, brush with beaten egg and bake in a moderate oven (350°F, 180°C, gas mark 4) for 1–1½ hours.

See photograph facing page 145

Farmhouse Game Pie

Small Game Pies

1lb (450g) diced cold game
gravy (see page 170)
a few mushrooms
shortcrust pastry (see page 164)

For the forcemeat

½lb (225g) suet
¼lb (100g) breadcrumbs
2oz (50g) chopped bacon
1 tablespoon chopped parsley
1 tablespoon chopped thyme
grated rind of 1 lemon
salt and pepper
1 egg, beaten

Make a forcemeat with the suet, breadcrumbs, chopped bacon, fresh parsley and thyme, some grated lemon rind, salt and pepper. Bind with the beaten egg.

Butter a pie dish, lay a strip of the pastry round the edge. Put in alternate layers of diced cold game and forcemeat (and add a few sliced mushrooms if available), pour in gravy, place a pie funnel in the centre, cover with short-crust pastry and bake in a moderate oven (350°F, 180°C, gas mark 4) for 1–1½ hours. *Serves 6.*

From time immemorial mince pies have had a place of honour at Christmas. Long before Christmas puddings became traditional, mince pies were regarded as part of the Christmas festivities. They were, however, of the savoury kind, and a fifteenth-century manuscript gives the recipe of that period:

'Take a pheasant, a hare, 2 pigeons and the kidneys of a sheep. Chop all together as fine as may be, add salt and pepper and spices, place in oval shaped crusts and bake well.'

A good way to use up left-over game oddments which should be very appetizing.

Incidentally, Pepys mentions that his wife sat up till four on Christmas morning, helping her maids make mince pies which, later in the day, he ate 'with plenty of good wine and a heart full of great joy'.

Part Three

Accompaniments to Fish and Game

Sauces are to cookery what grammar is
to language.

Alexis Soyer

Sauces

The object of serving sauce or gravy is to enhance the taste of the dish with which it is served, but whilst it should have a distinctive flavour this must not be overpowering. One culinary critic has claimed that a good cook may be known by his sauces but, after all, hunger is the best sauce.

With a few exceptions gravy is basically the juice of the meat or fish, roasted or braised in a baking dish, diluted if very thick and rich, or liquid and thickening added if the quantity is meagre. Having removed the joint, pour off all the fat (dripping) very carefully, retaining the sediment which usually includes rich brown particles. Pour in a little boiling water, put the tin over heat for a few minutes and stir and scrape till well mixed. Serve in a heated tureen, taking off any surplus fat which may rise to the top. If it is necessary to increase the quantity, mix two teaspoons of flour to a paste with a little cold water, make up to $\frac{1}{4}$ pint (150ml), then add gradually to the gravy till well blended. A little gravy browning will improve the colour, if this addition is necessary. My grandmother made her own colouring by burning a lump of sugar on a pattypan, held by fire-tongs close to the fire till well 'sizzled', and then plunging the little pan straight into the gravy.

The number of sauces is incalculable because it is inexhaustible, although I once read of a chef who claimed he made over 600 different kinds. Changing names, methods and ingredients make it impossible to give a comprehensive list, but by dividing and sub-dividing the aspiring cook can grasp the main trends.

Basically, of course, there is the division between savoury sauces and sweet sauces. Given the nature of this book we will be concerned exclusively with the former.

Convenience Gravy

Some joints, especially those frozen hard, do not exude a lot of gravy. One substitute, which looks and tastes very much like the real thing can be made by simmering 4 small onions, some sprigs of parsley and a bay leaf in just enough water to cover them. After about 40 minutes, strain, and boil the liquid again, adding a tablespoon of dripping, and a teaspoon of browning or beef extract. If necessary, thicken with a little flour blended to a paste with cold water.

Game Stock

The carcase of a game bird
the giblets (minus the liver)
2–3 carrots, cleaned and sliced
1 onion, peeled and stuck with 2–3 cloves
1–2 sticks celery, sliced
bouquet garni

Put the carcase, giblets, vegetables and *bouquet garni* in a large pan and cover them with water.

Bring slowly to the boil, remove any scum from the top, cover and simmer slowly for about 3 hours. Add more hot water if the liquid level should fall below the other ingredients.

Strain the stock through a fine sieve into a bowl. Remove the fat from the surface either by pulling absorbent paper across it or by allowing the stock to cool and the fat to settle in a layer which can be easily scooped off.

White and Cream Sauces

There are four – *béchamel, velouté,* espagnole, tomato – which can be split into the two kinds of white sauce, *béchamel* and *velouté*; the brown sauce (espagnole); and the tomato sauce (tomato).

Remember that, generally, white sauces and cream sauces are made with milk, *velouté* and brown and tomato sauces with stock. Divide again between the roux or paste method.

Then again, you can have a thin, medium or thick sauce. As a general guide, remember that for a thin *roux* sauce, you use 1oz (25g) flour and 1oz (25g) butter, oil or other fat to 1 pint (600ml) of liquid; half as much again of flour and fat for medium sauce; and for a thick sauce, 2oz (50g) flour, 2oz (50g) fat to the same 1 pint (600ml) of liquid. For the paste method, use 3 tablespoons of cornflour to 1 pint (600ml) of liquid for thin sauce, 4 tablespoons for medium and 5 tablespoons for thick sauce.

Béchamel Sauce

1½oz (40g) butter
1½oz (40g) flour
1pt (600ml) milk
salt and pepper

Melt the butter in a heavy saucepan over low heat. Stir in the flour with a wooden spoon. In another pan have ready the milk heated to boiling point. Cook the flour and butter mixture until it leaves the side of the pan (in about 2 minutes). This is now a white *roux*. Begin adding the boiling milk very slowly, stirring fast and always in the same direction. It is advisable to keep the pan away from the heat while adding the first half of the milk, but put it back when pouring in the rest and keep stirring until it boils. Turn the heat down, put a lid on to prevent a skin forming and let it simmer for another 15 minutes.

This is now ready for seasoning and using as it is or as a foundation for sauces of infinite variety and it is worth-while making a quantity and keeping it in an air-tight container in the refrigerator for use when needed in a hurry.

VARIATIONS

To make the following sauces, add the ingredients listed below. The quantities given are sufficient for 1 pint (600ml) *béchamel* sauce.

Anchovy Sauce

Blend a tablespoon of anchovy paste with a knob of butter and season to taste with lemon juice. *Serve with fish.*

Aurore Sauce

Flavour and colour to taste with tomato purée. *Serve with fish.*

Caper Sauce

Add 2 tablespoons capers, a tablespoon of chopped parsley and a little vinegar. *Serve with fish.*

Cheese Sauce

Add 2oz (50g) grated cheese, ½ teaspoon dry mustard and a pinch of cayenne pepper. *Serve with fish.*

Mornay Sauce

Add 2oz (50g) each grated Gruyère and Parmesan cheese, and a pinch of cayenne pepper. *Serve with fish.*

Onion Sauce

Add 2 large onions, boiled till tender, drained and chopped finely. (French chefs grate the onion raw and cook with the *béchamel* sauce.) *Serve with boiled fish.*

Piquant Sauce

Add 1 onion, 2 hard-boiled eggs, dill pickle and parsley, all finely minced. *Serve with fish.*

Velouté Sauce

This sauce is also made with a *roux* base, but the liquid added is white stock (fish, meat or vegetable) rather than milk. The following variations are made by adding the ingredients listed to 1 pint (600ml) *velouté* sauce.

Allemande Sauce

Make a thick *velouté* sauce with a *roux* from 2oz (50g) flour rather than 1½oz (40g). Blend 3 egg yolks and ¼ pint (150ml) cream together. Beat in some of the hot *velouté* sauce, then add this to the remainder. Bring slowly to the boil and boil for a few minutes. Season to taste with salt, pepper and lemon juice. *Serve with boiled or poached fish.*

Cardinal Sauce

Add ½ pint (300ml) fish fumet to 1 pint (600ml) *velouté* sauce and reduce to about ¾ pint (450ml). Add 2–3oz (50–75g) lobster or crab meat chopped very small.   *Serve with fish.*

Mustard Sauce

Add 2 teaspoons each of English and French made mustard and 2 tablespoons vinegar to 1 pint (600ml) *velouté* sauce made with fish fumet. Season with salt and pepper to taste. *Serve with fish.*

Poulette Sauce

Boil for a few minutes 1 pint (600ml) Allemande sauce. Add 4oz (100g) chopped mushrooms. Cook for 5 minutes more. Finish with 2oz (50g) chopped parsley, and a little lemon juice to taste.   *Serve with fish.*

Suprême Sauce

Beat 3 tablespoons double cream and 1 egg yolk well and add to 1 pint (600ml) *velouté* sauce. Pour into a bowl standing over a pan of simmering water. Stir until it has thickened, but do not allow to boil or the egg will curdle. Add lemon juice and butter and blend in. *Serve with fish.*

174 Start making this sauce as you would a *velouté*, but cook the butter and flour *roux* until it turns brown before adding stock. A little gravy browning or extract can help the good work. Variations are given below.

Barbecue Sauce

To 1 pint (600ml) Espagnole Sauce add 2 tablespoons each chopped parsley and chives, 1 tablespoon brown sugar, 2 tablespoons tarragon vinegar and a few drops of Worcestershire sauce. Season to taste with chilli powder or cayenne pepper. *Serve with game.*

Bordelais Sauce

Put 2oz (50g) chopped shallots or spring onions in a saucepan with $\frac{1}{2}$ pint (300ml) red wine. Reduce the wine by about three quarters and add $\frac{1}{2}$ pint (300ml) Espagnole sauce. *Serve with partridge.*

Chasseur Sauce

1pt (600ml) Espagnole sauce
2 shallots or small onions, finely chopped
1oz (25g) butter
6oz (75g) mushrooms, chopped
$\frac{1}{8}$pt (75ml) red wine
1 tablespoon brandy
1 tablespoon tomato purée
2 tablespoons chopped parsley

Make up the Espagnole sauce. Fry gently the shallots or spring onions in the butter until soft. Add the chopped mushrooms and sauté gently for a few minutes. Add the red wine, brandy, tomato purée and Espagnole Sauce. Simmer for 5 minutes. Season and stir in the chopped parsley. *Serve with roast duck.*

Poivrade Sauce

$\frac{1}{2}$pt (300ml) Espagnole sauce
2 shallots or 1 small onion
butter
$\frac{1}{2}$pt (300ml) red wine
$\frac{1}{8}$pt (75ml) red wine vinegar
12 crushed peppercorns

Cook the shallot or onion in a little butter until soft. Add to the wine and wine vinegar and boil until reduced by one third. Stir in the Espagnole sauce and simmer for about half an hour. Add the crushed peppercorns and simmer for another 10 minutes. Strain and reheat before serving and finish with a knob of butter. *Serve with venison or other game (particularly marinaded game).*

Note: If you serve this sauce with marinaded game, substitute $\frac{1}{2}$ pint (300ml) of the marinade in place of $\frac{1}{2}$ pint (300ml) red wine.

Robert Sauce

$\frac{1}{2}$pt (300ml) Espagnole sauce
1 large onion, minced
butter
$\frac{1}{4}$pt (150ml) dry white wine
3 tablespoons vinegar
2 teaspoons made mustard
pinch of caster sugar.

Fry the minced onion gently in a little butter until soft. Add the dry white wine and vinegar and reduce by half. Add the Espagnole sauce and simmer for 20 minutes. Stir in the mustard and caster sugar. *Serve with cold game.*

Apple Sauce

From Elizabeth Raffald's *The Experienced English Housekeeper* (1769)

1lb (450g) cooking apples
butter
sugar

Pare, core and slice your apples, put them in a saucepan, with as much water as will keep them from burning, set them over a slow fire, keep them close-covered till they are all of a pulp, then put in a lump of butter, and sugar to your taste, beat them well, and send them up to the table in a china basin. *Serve with wild duck and goose.*

Bread Sauce

1 small onion, stuck with 3 cloves
¾pt (450ml) milk
4oz (100g) fresh breadcrumbs
nutmeg
salt and white pepper
1oz (25g) butter
2 tablespoons cream

Put the onion and milk in a saucepan and bring slowly to boiling point. Remove from the heat and leave to infuse for about 20 minutes.

Remove the onion and stir in the breadcrumbs until they are well absorbed. Stir in the seasonings, butter and cream and heat through. If it seems too thick add a little more milk, if too thin, more crumbs. *Serve with pheasant and other wild fowl.*

Cherry Sauce

1lb (450g) stoned cherries
½pt (300ml) claret
2 tablespoons redcurrant jelly
the peel of 1 lemon
2oz (50g) caster sugar
a glass of kirsch

Put the stoned cherries in a saucepan with the claret, redcurrant jelly, lemon peel and caster sugar. Bring to the boil, then simmer for about 30 minutes. Remove the lemon peel and set aside the sauce to cool. Just before serving add the glass of kirsch. *Serve with venison, wild duck or goose.*

Cider Sauce

1 rasher of fat bacon, finely chopped
1 onion, finely chopped
½pt (300ml) cider
2 tablespoons cornflour
1 teaspoon honey

Put the chopped rasher and onion in a saucepan with the cider. Boil for 30 minutes. Strain and return the liquid to the saucepan. Blend the cornflour with 2 tablespoons cold water, pour a little of the hot liquid on to mix well, then add to the rest of the liquid. Stir in the honey and boil again for another 2–3 minutes. *Serve with venison, roast duck or goose.*

Colette Sauce

green tops of a few sticks of celery
parsley
two hard-boiled egg yolks
4 tablespoons olive oil
2 tablespoons wine vinegar
1 teaspoon French mustard
salt and freshly ground black pepper

Wash and finely chop the green tops of celery with an equal amount of parsley. Pound the hard-boiled egg yolks and put in a bowl with the celery and parsley. Add slowly the olive oil, wine vinegar and mustard. Season to taste with salt and black pepper. *Serve with fish.*

This recipe was recommended by an American friend, who in turn acquired it from a French chef. She claims it is quite as nice as mayonnaise and much easier to make.

Curry Sauce

3 tablespoons desiccated coconut
½pt (300ml) milk
2 onions, chopped
butter
1 apple, peeled and sliced
2 tomatoes, skinned and chopped
2 teaspoons curry powder
salt
½pt (300ml) white wine
cream

Put the desiccated coconut to soak in the milk. Fry the chopped onion in the butter until soft. Add the sliced apple, skinned and chopped tomatoes, curry powder and salt to taste. Cook slowly until tender. Add the white wine, the milk and coconut. Simmer for 30 minutes. Put through a sieve, add a little cream and reheat. *Use with anything suitable for a curry.*

Cranberry Sauce

Put ½lb (225g) cranberries, and 6oz (175g) sugar in a saucepan with ¼ pint (150ml) water. Bring to the boil, cover and cook gently for about 10 minutes or until the skins break. Leave to get cold. *Serve with game.*

Cumberland Sauce

1 orange
1 lemon
½lb (225g) redcurrant jelly
1 teaspoon French mustard
⅛pt (75ml) port wine
ground ginger
salt and pepper

Peel the orange and lemon thinly, cut it into matchstick-sized strips and blanch in boiling water. Drain and set aside. Heat the redcurrant jelly and mustard over gentle heat, blending well. Add the juice of the orange and lemon, the ginger, salt and pepper. Stir in the peel and simmer for 5 minutes. *Serve cold with venison and other game, duck or goose.*

Hollandaise Sauce

6oz (175g) butter, cut into 12 pieces
2 tablespoons lemon juice
2 tablespoons white wine vinegar
1 tablespoon water
3 egg yolks
salt and pepper

Cut the butter into 12 pieces. Put the lemon juice, vinegar and water into a small saucepan and boil until the liquid is reduced to only 2 tablespoons. Put into a bowl and leave to cool. Beat the egg yolks into the reduced liquid and set this over a pan of barely simmering water on a low heat. Add the butter piece by piece, adding the next piece only when the last one has been whisked in and well absorbed. The sauce is ready when all the butter has been added and the sauce itself is thick enough to coat the back of a spoon. Check seasoning and serve. *Serve with fish, particularly salmon, sea trout and trout.*

Horseradish Cream Sauce

2 tablespoons finely grated horseradish
1 teaspoon wine vinegar
½ teaspoon caster sugar
salt and pepper
¼pt (150ml) double cream

Mix together the horseradish, vinegar and caster sugar. Season lightly with salt and pepper and gently fold in the cream. *Serve with roast game, hot or cold salmon or smoked fish.*

Maître d'Hôtel Butter

As this is such a useful accompaniment to many dishes it is worth while making it in some quantity, forming it into a cylindrical piece and storing it, foil-wrapped, in the refrigerator. You can then cut off neat roundels as required.

Soften ½lb (225g) unsalted butter slightly and cream it in a mixing bowl with finely chopped parsley, and lemon juice to taste. *Serve with fish and grilled game.*

Montpelier Butter

8oz (225g) softened butter
6 anchovies, pounded
1 tablespoon each capers, minced parsley, chives and tarragon
freshly ground black pepper

Cream the pounded anchovies, capers, minced herbs, and freshly ground pepper into the softened butter. Store as *maître d'hôtel* butter above. *Serve with coarse fish.*

Mayonnaise

To make ½ pint (300ml)

3 egg yolks
½ teaspoon salt
½ teaspoon dry mustard
1 tablespoon lemon juice or wine vinegar
½pt (300ml) olive oil

Put the egg yolks in a mixing bowl with the salt and beat until thick. Add the mustard and lemon juice and stir in. Add the oil, drop by drop, beating continuously. After about one third of the oil has been added you can speed up the process and add the rest in a thin stream. When all the oil has been absorbed, stir in 1 tablespoon boiling water to prevent curdling, and check seasoning.

VARIATIONS

Andalouse

To ½ pint (300ml) mayonnaise add 4 tablespoons tomato purée and add 2 small pimentos, chopped finely. *Serve with fish.*

Chive Mayonnaise Sauce

To the basic mayonnaise add as much finely chopped chives as you wish. *Serve with fish, particularly cold salmon and lobster.*

Niçoise

Add a clove of crushed garlic, 2 tablespoons finely chopped green olives (or gherkins) and a teaspoon of lemon juice to ½ pint (300ml) mayonnaise. *Serve with fish.*

Rémoulade

To ½ pint (300ml) mayonnaise add 1½ teaspoons Dijon mustard and 2 tablespoons of mixed chopped capers, chives, gherkins and parsley. *Serve with fish.*

Tartare Sauce

Make up ½ pint (300ml) mayonnaise, but using hard-boiled egg yolks. Stir in 3 tablespoons each finely chopped gherkins and capers and 1 tablespoon finely chopped parsley. *Serve with fish.*

Thousand Island

Remove the seeds from a green pepper, cook it in boiling water for 5 minutes and chop finely. Add, together with 2 teaspoons chilli sauce and a few drops of brandy, to ½ pint (300ml) mayonnaise. *Serve with shellfish.*

Orange Sauce

In the early years of this century, duck was invariably served with sage and onion stuffing and apple sauce (see page 175), but since then orange sauce has become more popular, although in France it had mostly been served with white fish. Methods of making it vary considerably, but I have found this one to be very good.

1 orange
¼pt (150ml) cream
¼pt (150ml) white wine
1 teaspoon lemon juice
2 egg yolks
2oz (50g) unsalted butter
pinch of cayenne pepper
small tin of mandarin oranges (optional)

Grate the rind of the orange and set it aside. Squeeze the juice into a bowl. Add to this the cream, white wine, lemon juice and the egg yolks. Put into a double boiler and heat, whisking continuously, until it thickens smoothly. Beat in the unsalted butter, cut into pieces, and add the reserved grated orange rind and a pinch of cayenne pepper. A tin of mandarin oranges can be drained and the segments used for garnish.

Alternatively, you can make the sauce the easy way, using the same tin of mandarins. First separate the fruit from the juice. Make up the latter to ½ pint (300ml) with fresh orange juice and a squeeze of lemon. Add the grated rind of an orange. Mix a heaped teaspoon of arrowroot with a little water, stir in and cook until the sauce thickens. Then add the mandarin segments.

Ravigote Sauce

Mix five parts olive oil with two parts vinegar and a little mustard to make a vinaigrette base. Add to this minced shallots, parsley, chives and season with salt and pepper. *Serve with boiled fish.*

Red Wine Sauce

½pt (300ml) beef stock
1 tablespoon redcurrant jelly
¼pt (150ml) port wine
salt and pepper

Melt the redcurrant jelly into the beef stock over a low heat. Stir in the port wine and season with salt and pepper. *Serve with venison, game birds and pigeon.*

Sage and Onion Sauce

2 tablespoons butter
2 minced onions
½pt (300ml) game stock (see page 170)
1 teaspoon finely chopped sage

Melt the butter in a saucepan and gently brown the onions in it. Add the stock, bring to the boil, then add the sage and season to taste. *Serve with roast duck and game birds.*

Savoie

5oz (150g) shelled walnuts
½pt (300ml) cream
5oz (150g) grated horseradish
2 tablespoons white breadcrumbs
2 teaspoons caster sugar
1 teaspoon lemon juice
pinch of salt

Remove the brown skin from the shelled walnuts (boiling water poured over will make it easy to rub the skin off). Chop them finely. Mix together the cream, grated horseradish, breadcrumbs, caster sugar, lemon juice and a pinch of salt, and add the walnuts to this.

This was Escoffier's sauce to serve with salmon and trout.

White Wine Sauce

4 tablespoons white wine
3 tablespoons vinegar
1 large onion, chopped
a few anchovies, chopped
¼pt (150ml) thick cream

Simmer the onion and anchovies in the white wine and vinegar for about 30 minutes, then strain. Add the thick cream and stir over low heat to amalgamate. *Serve with fish, particularly salmon.*

Reform Club Sauce

2 tablespoons wine vinegar
2 tablespoons caster sugar
1 tablespoon crushed black peppercorns
1 onion, finely chopped
½pt good stock
1 tablespoon redcurrant jelly
2 tablespoons beetroot ⎫ very
2 tablespoons gherkin ⎬ thinly
2 tablespoons hardboiled white of egg ⎭ sliced

Put the vinegar, sugar, crushed peppercorns and onion into a pan and cook slowly until the onion is soft then add the stock and redcurrant jelly and go on cooking gently for another 5 minutes. Strain, then add to the liquor the remaining ingredients. Bring to the boil and serve.

Unfortunately, I haven't any of Soyer's books, but I cherish this one recipe because it reminds me that, in a world so full of selfishness, greed and corruption, there are men and women who will travel far afield to help their fellow men:

In 1855, Alexis Soyer, a little Frenchman absorbed in his art of cookery overheard members of the Reform Club discussing the appalling disaster of the decimation of the Light Brigade in that famous charge. He felt the urge to help and finally obtained grudging permission to go to the Crimea. So he left the distinguished Club and joined Florence Nightingale at Scutari, coping with dirt, disease and facing death in primitive conditions with inadequate materials; his only reward was the gratitude of those he served. He returned to England in 1857, worn out, and died a few months later.

Wine

The subtle alchemist that, in a trice,
Life's leaden metal into gold transmutes.
Omar Khayyam

One could write volumes on the subject of wines and spirits, beer and cider, cordials, punches, etc., but on this topic, I am no authority. I don't like ale, beer or lager, and spirits don't like me.

For centuries, wine has been made at home, and, in recent years, numerous wine clubs have sprung up, a hobby leading to happy and healthy friendships through a common interest. Now home brewing and wine-making kits are obtainable from chemists and stores, but anyone indulging in such activities should remember that their productions are much more potent than the mass-produced variety, having a far stronger alcoholic content, which could be lethal for a driver.

Far down the ages, we have seen the tragic results of over-indulgence in strong drink, going right back to Noah, who, before the Flood had 'found grace in the eyes of the Lord'. He started off a new world by planting a vineyard, making wine from the grapes and finally becoming a drunkard.

And because his son Ham found him in a debauched state, he became vicious and vindictive and he (described as 'a just man') punished poor innocent Ham by laying a curse on Ham's son, Canaan. Incidentally, it is interesting to learn that when Ham told his brothers, Shem and Japeth, of their father's shocking state, they took clothing in to cover him, walking backwards with their eyes averted. Evidently, the forerunners of our diplomats and politicians.

And some generations after, there was the story of Abraham's nephew, Lot, who was not a total abstainer:

Old wine-loving Lot
Drinking tot after tot
Found himself in a spot
Slept all through the night, he believed;
But learned he had not,
When he discovered just what,
Was his part in the plot,
His two daughters conceived.

There is, of course, nothing whatever wrong with alcohol; indeed, scientists have agreed that wine is, in fact, a food with a well-marked action on the nervous system. Claret and similar wines are digestive agents of a high order, valuable remedies for anaemia and weight loss and aids to convalescence after illness, while champagne is a restorer from any exhaustion. Louis Pasteur claimed, '*Un repas sans vin est un jour sans soleil,*' while Alfred Noyes became lyrical on the subject:

Wine, mellow and deep as the sunset,
With mirth in it, singing as loud
As the skylark sings in a high wind,
High over a crisp white cloud.

Like most things, consumption of wine has a humorous side. We now have a new type of comedian, the wine snob. And, this is a serious matter for Women's Lib. Why does a wine waiter always proffer the wine list to a man, if one is present? And, if no other male is there, why does the one usually order without any reference to his lady friend? The waiter appears with a bottle and shows the label. The gentleman takes a look and may make a knowing remark regarding the quality, maturity and the vintage. Some wine is then poured for the tasting ceremony. First, the host will pass the glass to and fro under his delicate nostrils (questing like a hound for the scent), then he will sip just enough to reach his taste buds, adopting a pensive meditative expression, after which he will incline his head gracefully and with dignity, while admiring females let out the breath they have been holding. And there is the show-off who will complain that the white wine is not sufficiently chilled or the red wine is not *chambré*.

Generally, the wine snob has far less real discernment than those he is trying to impress, but he probably knows someone 'in the trade', belongs to a wine society, goes to wine-tasting parties and wine auctions and studies the *World Atlas of Wine*, thereby gathering sufficient information to get by. Some time ago, I read of such a man who was dining with his brother-in-law. The latter had somehow acquired an empty Château Margaux bottle, which he filled with 'plonk' from a supermarket, and when the know-all gentleman had put on the usual performance of sniffing, tasting and eye-rolling, he congratulated his host and went on, 'Superb bouquet, my boy, one can almost taste the violets.'

On the rare occasion when I'm acting as hostess at a restaurant and the question of wine choice is left to me, I remember Robert Morley, who once said, 'Not being a connoisseur of wine, I usually leave it to the wine waiter to unload on me what he wants to dispose of. That way, at least one of us is satisfied.'

Red wine is supposed to be served at room (*chambré*) temperature (experts say 60°F is ideal). Clarets can be a few degrees higher and the corks should be drawn an hour or two before drinking to allow the wine to 'breathe'. It's a good idea to put the wine glasses with the bottles to acquire the same temperature.

Rosé wines should be served cold like white wine, while both sherry and tawny port are best cooled. Champagne should be iced.

Traditionalists drink white wine with fish, red wine with meat and game and sweet white wine with dessert. In the last century and early part of the present, a different wine was served with each of the six or seven courses of a meal and even after that, when the ladies retired, port was solemnly passed round the table until disposed of.

In 1861 Mrs Beeton wrote:

In former times, when the bottle circulated freely among the guests, it was necessary for the ladies to retire earlier than they do at present, for the gentlemen of the company soon became unfit to conduct themselves with that decorum which is essential in modern Society. Temperance is, in these happy days, a striking feature in the character of a gentleman.

One cannot help wondering what improvements Mrs Beeton would find in *our* modern society.

A gallant major whom I used to know always claimed that it was a mistake to mix any wine during dinner. 'Whatever you begin with,' he used to say, 'drink throughout the meal.' Generally speaking, however, I have found that if guests have sherry or an aperitif before dinner, they like white wine with fish and enjoy red wine with meat or game, but the amount should be limited to one glass for each course, unless the food is to become floating islands in a stomach awash. Just as a topper-up, a liqueur or a little cognac with coffee is permissible.

But tastes differ and fashions change in wines. If you are entertaining old friends, you know their likes and dislikes, but if you have guests of whose preferences you are not aware, it is best to be candid and say what wine you are proposing to serve with the fish and what with the game (I don't believe in serving a third wine with dessert – that is just gilding the lily), and then ask what sort of aperitif they would like. Ninety per cent plump for sherry, but you do get an occasional Philistine who demands whisky and soda, gin and vermouth or Campari.

A dry white wine like Pouilly Fuissé goes very well with fish and shellfish, but if a rich sauce is an accompaniment, the even drier Pouilly Fumé is better. In Normandy, a light white wine, Muscadet or Meursault is sometimes served with roast chicken, although a full-bodied Alsace Riesling is equally suitable. For game, the heavier red wines, such as clarets and burgundies or a Rhône wine like Châteauneuf-du-Pape, are best.

If, as has often happened in my home, friends stay on until the small hours, they will need an occasional light snack and refreshing drink. A glass of champagne is always welcome, but a cheap alternative is Asti Spumante, which has an energizing sparkle. Its alcoholic content is low, but it needs to be served very cold. (For those who like sweet wine, there is an alternative called Asti Barbero.)

Appendix

Home Freezing of Fish and Game

186 Trout, sea-trout, salmon, eels and grayling will keep for at least twelve months in excellent condition if the following procedure is adopted:

As soon as possible after catching and killing the fish, put it in a very cool place. An insulated box containing 'freeze packs' or plastic bottles filled with water or, better still, car anti-freeze, and frozen, is suitable, or you can use a space-blanket, obtainable from camping equipment shops, to enclose fish and frozen packs or bottles.

If fish can be put into this kind of cold-store very soon after being caught, they can be enclosed in plastic tubing, obtainable from Lakeland Plastics Ltd, Alexandra Road, Windermere, Westmorland, knotted at each end. As much air as possible should be squeezed out before tying the second knot.

If there is unavoidable delay, never put fish in a plastic or rubberized bag. Use a fishmonger's bass-bag. Only put the fish into plastic tubing immediately before they go into the cold-box or space-blanket, or direct into the freezer.

Squeeze out excreta by running finger and thumb down the lower abdomen of the fish, before bagging and cooling. Wipe off any blood, sand, soil, grass or leaves.

Do not gut the fish, scale it, or cut it in any way, if you want it to keep in the freezer as long as possible. Where a whole fish will keep twelve months, a gutted or cut fish will keep only three or four months. If you cut a big trout or salmon into steaks before freezing, use them within three months.

Do not coat the fish with a layer of ice by repeated dips in water after freezing. It will not keep any longer, and you will have a wet mess when you thaw it. Ice-coating is often recommended but has no advantage over plastic tubing.

There are various estimates of how long fish can be kept deep-frozen. Generally, if frozen whole, salmon, salmon trout, brown and rainbow trout can be kept for twelve months, though some flavour is lost after six to eight months. Fresh salmon steaks deteriorate more rapidly and should not be kept frozen for more than six to eight weeks.

If you have frozen a large salmon whole, you can saw off steaks. Use a carpenter's rip-saw; hacksaws, tenon saws and special knives supposed to cut frozen meat are all useless. But once you have cut the fish, you must use it all up in three months or so.

Everyone knows that if a fish has been frozen and then thawed it must not be re-frozen without first being cooked. But if a big trout or salmon has been frozen whole, it can be thawed, salted and cold-smoked, which will produce two sides. These can be re-frozen and will keep for about three months in the case of smoked salmon and nine months or more in the case of smoked trout. If you intend to re-freeze cold smoked fish, leave the bones in for maximum storage time. This is not very convenient if you have a pair of large smoked sides, since it takes a party of twenty to thirty people to eat the smoked side of a 10lb (5 kg) salmon or trout. So you can remove the bones and slice the side, freezing the slices in little packs of 4oz (100g) each. These will keep for four months or more, and you can remove and thaw them when needed, allowing a 4oz (100g) pack for two people.

Fish should be thawed slowly in the unopened packaging. When you remove a whole fish from the freezer, keep an eye on it while it is thawing. If you catch it at the right time during the thawing period, you can remove the guts in one solid, odourless, frozen chunk, saving much trouble and mess. But before gutting the fish, put it into a bowl of salt water and scrub off the slime with a coarse cloth or a scrubbing brush. You shouldn't have done that before freezing; the natural slime when frozen helps to prevent loss of flavour, but you don't want it on the fish while it is being cooked. This is especially important with trout caught from lakes.

Shellfish of all kinds are best frozen immediately after catching and cooking, although oysters and mussels are occasionally frozen raw after opening and cleaning.

Eels can be stewed or jellied, and will keep for twelve months when frozen.

Smoked fish also freezes well. Rub each fish well with salad oil before packing and freezing, as this will prevent the surface drying out when thawing.

If these are to be hung, this should be done before freezing. With water birds, freshness is paramount, so hanging time should be minimal. Any fish content in the intestine can contaminate the flesh, which intensifies with freezing. After preparation (see below) freeze immediately. Delay causes deterioration during storage.

Birds should be plucked before freezing and any visible shot or badly broken bones removed, but it is perhaps better not to draw them – not because they keep any better undrawn, but because, as with fish, you can catch then when partly thawed and get the guts out in a frozen lump, thereby avoiding mess and smells. Leave the head on however until the bird is thawed.

Age is important. Freeze young birds for roasting, etc. Older birds can first be pressure-cooked and the meat removed from the bones, and then frozen for use in casseroles, game pies, etc. The bones can be stewed, strained, and the resulting stock frozen separately. It is a great pity to waste it. An old pheasant or duck can be minced and, if necessary, eked out by adding minced veal or pork, and then made into a shepherd's pie with the usual crust of mashed potato. A pinch of mixed herbs, half a glass of sherry and a dash of Worcestershire sauce will make this into a delicious dish.

Game birds will keep about twelve months in a deep-freeze but begin to lose some flavour after about six months.

Preparation of game for freezing

Remove the oil sack from the base of the tail of game birds. The retained giblets must be wrapped in polythene or foil separately from the bird. *Never* store these in the cavity as the storage life is only two months compared with the twelve months or so for uncooked game.

If freezing large quantities, chill between preparing and freezing.

All bone protrusions must be padded before packing, using foil or greaseproof paper. Carefully mould the foil or other wrapping around the bird, expelling the air. Cover completely and seal by twisting the foil or securing with special freezer tape. As foil punctures easily, protect it by overwrapping in a thin polythene bag or a piece of muslin cloth.

Labelling

Do not forget to label each item clearly, noting the type of game, its weight and the date of freezing. Use special freezer labels and write on them only with waterproof pens or pencils.

Hang these by the head, with a container to catch the blood, which can be frozen separately in a carton.

Hares and rabbits must be skinned, gutted and put into air-tight bags before freezing. They can be frozen whole or cut into joints or portions, which will keep in the deep freeze for about twelve to eighteen months.

If you want to freeze rabbits for your cats or dogs, it saves space if you pressure cook the rabbits, remove the meat from the bones and cut it up small, pressing it into plastic containers in which cream and yoghourt are supplied. The filled containers can be frozen all together in large plastic bags.

Note: Fish for cats can be treated in a similar way. Take care to remove all bones from pet foods of this sort.

Venison

After beheading, clean the carcase carefully, then skin and bleed it. Hang in a very cold place, with the belly well open to allow air to circulate. Seven to ten days' hanging should be enough, and during this time the carcase should be wiped over with milk every other day to help keep the meat in good condition.

The prime joints can be frozen whole wrapped in polythene, and the rest of the meat minced and frozen raw, or casseroled and made into game pies and then frozen.

Index

Allemande sauce, 173
anchovy sauce, 172
angels on horseback, 46
anglers, advice to, 62
anguilles, *see* eels
apple sauce, 175
aurore sauce, 172

barbecue sauce, 174
barbel:
   baked, 71
   poached, 71
béchamel sauce, 21, 172
blackcock, 116
Bordelais sauce, 174
bouillabaisse, freshwater,
   76
bread sauce, 175
bream:
   baked, 72
   baked fillets with bacon,
      72
   baked with oysters and
      lemon, 72
   bakemeat, 73
   boiled, 72
   plaki, 73
brochet, *see* pike
Brunswick Stew, 156
Bumper Bushytail, 157

caille, *see* quail
canard, *see* duck
caper sauce, 172
capercailzie, 115:
   casseroled, 115
cardinal sauce, 173
carp, 56–7:
   à Fleuve, 60
   baked, 58
   Cardinal, 58
   Curé's omelette, 61
   Florentine fillets, 61
   Izaak Walton's way, 59
   Portugaise, 60

spiced baked, 59
stuffed, 58 *see also* pike
ceviche, 90
char, 74:
   fried, 74
   potted, 74
chasseur sauce, 174
cheese sauce, 172
cherry sauce, 175
chub, 75:
   stewed, 75
cider sauce, 175
clam chowder, 53
Colette sauce, 176
coquilles, *see* scallops
crab:
   devilled, 44
   dressed, 43
   mousse, 43
   sauce, 40
   soufflé, 44
   see also crayfish, lobster
cranberry sauce, 176
crayfish:
   bateaux d'écrevisses,
      45
   cocktail, 45 *see also* crab,
      lobster
cream sauce, 171
Cumberland sauce, 176
curry sauce, 176

dace:
   potted, 78
   spiced, 78
deer, 138–9
deer, recipes for, *see* venison
draining (game), 104
duck, 124:
   Candide, 125
   Épicé, 126
   flambé à l'eau de vie, 125
   Morena, 126
   roast, 124 *see also* goose,
      teal, widgeon

écrevisses, *see* crayfish
eels, 92:
   au vert, 97
   catigau d'anguilles, 97
   cuisine d'amour, 95
   freezing methods, 186
   Izaak Walton's recipe, 98
   matelote of, 96
   pie, 94
   Pytchley stewed, 96
   skinning of, 92–3
   smoked, 35
   smoked, Smetana, 36
   souced, 93 *see also* Elvers
egg and salmon patties, 35
eggs, buttered, with salmon,
   34
elvers:
   fried, 98
   omelette, 98 *see also* eels
Espagnole sauces, 174

faison, *see* pheasant
fish:
   à la Portugaise, 87
   bubble and squeak, 77
   keeping fresh, methods
      of, 14
   mould, 86
   mousse, 88
   pie, 89
   savoury supper, 88
   smoked, 32–3
   soufflé, 88
   with curry, 87
Florentine fillets, 61
flounder:
   baked, 79
   filet Duglere, 79
freezing:
   fish, 186
   game birds, 187–8
   hares, 188
   rabbits, 188
   venison, 188

190 game, draining of, 104
game birds, freezing methods,
  187
game casserole, 161
game pies, 164–8:
  Devonshire game pie, 167
  farmhouse game pie, 168
  Fred Taylor's game pie,
   166
  Pytchley game pie, 167
  Welsh game pie, 167
game puddings, 165
game soufflé, 163
game with potatoes, 160
goose:
  à cidre, 129
  Yorkshire pie, 130
gousse, see goose
gravy, 170
grayling:
  aux noisettes, 81
  baked, 80
  freezing methods, 186
  Gaillard, 81
  stuffed, 80
grouse, 113:
  à la Georgienne, 113
  roast with brandy sauce, 113
  spatchcock, 114
  Swedish, 114
gudgeon, deep fried, 82

hanging:
  deer, 140
  game, 102
  venison, 140
hare, 146:
  freezing methods, 188
  hongroise, 149
  jugged, 148
  paunching, 147
  pudding, 150
  roasted, 149
  saddle of, with chestnuts,
   150

  skinning, 147
  Suisse, 150
  trussing, 147 see also rabbit
hash supreme, 162
Hollandaise sauce, 177
homard, see lobster
Horseradish cream sauce, 177

landrail, 122
lièvre, see hare
lobster, 38:
  à l'Américaine, 41
  à la Greque, 40
  au Gratin, 42
  Bisque, 42
  mousse, 40
  Newburg, 39
  ramekins, 40
  sauce, 40
  Thermidor, 39 see also
   crab, crayfish

maître d'hôtel butter, 177
mayonnaise, 178
Montpelier butter, 177
mornay sauce, 172
moules, see mussels
mousse:
  crab, 42
  fish, 88
  lobster, 40
  smoked fish, 34
mullet, baked, 83
mussels, 49:
  à la Poulette, 49
  marinières, 49 see also clams,
   oysters, scallops
mustard sauce, 173

onion sauce, 172
orange sauce, 179
Oregon tart, 165
Otak-Otak, 30
oysters, 46:
  angels on horseback, 46

  au gratin, 46 see also clams,
   mussels, scallops

parsley sauce, 17
partridge, 111:
  à chou rouge, 112
  au choux, 112
  grilled, 111
  roast, 111
pastry, savoury shortcrust, 164
patti casserole, 162
paunching:
  hares, 147
  rabbits, 151
pelotas, 163
perch, 84:
  stuffed baked, 84
pheasant, 107:
  à la Normande, 109
  Alcantara, 109
  au Verger, 109
  diable, 109
  grilled, 110
  roast, 107
  salmis de, 110
  stuffings for, 108 see also
   grouse, partridge
pigeon, 132:
  à la Française, 135
  en Escabèche, 133
  fried, 133
  grilled, 133
  Hertfordshire casserole, 135
  pie, 133, 134
  pudding, 136
  roast, 132
  stewed, 133
pike, 63–4:
  baked, 65
  boiled, 65
  casserole, 67
  collared, 67
  de Vouvray, 66
  fingers à la Vasconcellos, 68
  fried, 65

192 trout—*cont.*
    smoked, mousse 34
    smoking methods, 32–3
truite, *see* trout
trussing:
    game, 104
    hares, 147

velouté sauces, 173
venison:
    à Franche, 144

casserole, 143
freezing methods,
    188
French pie, 142
hanging, 140
roast, 141
steaks, 142
viande à hiver, 161

water souchy, 77
white sauce, 171

white wine sauce, 180
widgeon, 127
    roast, 127
wild duck, *see* duck
wild goose, *see* goose
wine, 181–3
woodcock, 118:
    boiled, 118
    casserole, 119
    roast, 119 *see also* plover,
        quail, snipe

Lyonnaise, Escoffier's, 66

Vermont, 66 *see also* carp

piquant sauce, 172

plover, 120:

aux olives, 120

plucking (game), 104

pluvier, *see* plover

poisson flambeau, 26

poivrade sauce, 174

poulette sauce, 173

prawns, 50:

cocktail, 50

curried 51

pancakes, 52

Tennessee pilaff, 52

see also scampi, shrimps

ptarmigan, 116

quail, 121:

à la Dauphine, 121

with apple, 121

rabbit, 151, 155

farmhouse, 155

freezing methods, 188

Galantine, 154

German stewed, 153

Hunters pie, 154

pudding, 155

roast, 152

skins, 147

Spanish stewed, 153 *see also* Hare

ravigote sauce, 179

red wine sauce, 179

Reform Club sauce, 180

roach:

baked, 85

boiled, 85

Robert sauce, 174

rolypoly:

baked, 165

family (boiled), 165

rook pie, 136

sage and onion sauce, 179

salade morceau, 34

salmon, 16:

baked, 19

boyled, 18

coquille of, 21

coulibiac, 20

freezing methods, 186

grilled, 19

in a basket, 22

Jack Thorndike's recipe, 17

kedgeree, 21

potted, 22

roasted, 18

ragoût, 20

smoked, *see* smoked salmon

soufflé, 22

steamed, 19

sweet-sour, 21 *see also* sea trout, smoked salmon

sauces, 170–80

savoie, 180

scalloped fish, 86

scallops, 47:

buttered, 48

preparation of, 47

Saint-Jacques à la Provençale 47

Stafford, 48 *see also* clams, mussels, oysters

scampi, 50:

Provençale, 53 *see also* prawns, shrimps

sea trout:

hot baked, 23

in rosé wine jelly, 24

with avocado sauce, 23

see also trout

shrimps, 50:

tomatoes, stuffed with, 53

Vermont, 52 *see also* prawns, scampi

singeing (game), 104

skinning:

hares, 147

rabbits, 147

smoked eels, *see* Eels, smoked

smoked salmon:

canapés, 35

methods of smoking, 32–3

mousse, 34

patties with egg, 34

salade morceau, 34

soufflé, 34

with buttered eggs, 34

snipe, 120:

boiled, 118

Italian, 120

soufflé:

crab, 44

fish, 88

game, 163

salmon, 22

spatchcock, 114

squirrel, 156:

Brunswick stew, 156

Bumper Bushytail, 157

stuffings, roast pheasant, 108

suprême sauce, 173

teal, 127

tench, stewed, 85

Tennessee pilaff, 52

trout, 25:

au bleu, 26

baked, Mrs Beeton's, 28

Barker's pie, 29

chamonix, 30

freezing methods, 186

Genevoise, 29

Guichen, 26

in aspic, 30

Jurassienne, 27

Mursley, 28

Otak-Otak, 30

Père Louis, 26

poretta, 27

sea trout, 23